THE ROADMAP I NEVER HAD

The Roadmap I Never Had

Continuing the Real Work Before, During, and After College Sports

Morgan Stuart

Published by Game Changer Publishing

Paperback ISBN: 979-8-90158-006-6

Hardcover ISBN: 979-8-90158-007-3

Digital ISBN: 979-8-90158-008-0

www.GameChangerPublishing.com

For the student-athletes.
Own your moment and be better than we were.

READ THIS FIRST

To thank you for being here, I want to give you access to my free community so you can share your story and learn from others as they navigate failure, pressure, and more. The community also has courses and tools. They're here whenever you need them.

Scan the QR Code Here:

THE ROADMAP I NEVER HAD

CONTINUING THE REAL WORK BEFORE, DURING, AND AFTER COLLEGE SPORTS

MORGAN STUART

FOREWORD

May 29, 2011, I called the game on ESPN between Missouri and Washington that would end Morgan Stuart's college softball career.

Before the game, she was one of the chosen players. I interviewed her at the team hotel. She was calm, thoughtful, well-spoken, methodical. Everything you'd expect from a senior playing in the postseason, knowing every game might be her final game. I remember thinking she seemed ready—composed in a way that stood out from other players I had interviewed.

I had no idea what was actually going through her head.

I didn't know she was numb. I didn't know she'd spent four years learning to turn off her feelings just to survive the pressure. I didn't know that when she got that hit up the middle in her last at-bat, standing on first base looking up at her mom, she felt insignificant instead of proud. I didn't know she'd walk off that field feeling like her career had amounted to nothing.

I didn't know because she was doing what every athlete learns to do: look fine on the outside while struggling on the inside.

That game was just the beginning of *knowing* Morgan.

A few years after that, we traveled the country together with the Packaged Deal—a group of former college softball players putting on clinics all over the United States. I coached pitching; she, of course, taught defense. We spent endless hours in cars, on planes, in hotels, planning clinics and getting to know each other on a deeper level.

Morgan was brilliant at teaching defense, but there was always something more driving her work with athletes—something she was trying to understand. Something that went well beyond the mechanics and drills I watched her show up and teach for hours on end. It was apparent to me there was always something pulling at her... motivating her... driving her.

After the crazy travel of the Packaged Deal ended due to COVID, I watched her go inward and do the hard work of understanding what she'd been through—both during her time at Washington and in the years leading up to it.

For the past five years, I've seen her pursue this mission: the mental side of being a competitive athlete, the stuff nobody wants to talk about. It's been inside her all along, but she had to work through it herself before she could write it down for others. This book isn't just helpful for athletes. It's been necessary for her.

Morgan's voice matters because she's not writing theory. She lived every bit of this. The perfectionism. The weight gain nobody talks about. The isolation that makes everything worse. The moment you realize you've been acting "fine" for so long that you've forgotten how to actually feel anything. She'll tell you about all of it—the unflattering parts, the mistakes, the things athletes are supposed to pretend don't happen.

She's also worked with thousands of athletes since her playing career ended, and she's seen these same patterns repeat. The high school players panicking about recruiting because their friends are committing to DI schools. The freshmen who think being prepared means having everything figured out before they arrive on campus. The college athletes playing scared, hesitant, distracted by fear of failure. The seniors who end their careers feeling relief instead of pride.

Every year, I call over 100 games on TV across professional, college, and Little League levels of softball. I see it constantly. Athletes performing below their ability because they're playing scared. Young players comparing themselves to everyone else on social media, convinced their worth is tied to a scholarship offer. The statistics and the highlight plays tell one story, but if you're paying attention, you can see what's happening beneath the surface.

Here's what makes this urgent: athletes are struggling in silence right now, and that silence doesn't just make college harder. It sets them up for a lifetime of tying their worth to performance, not knowing how to process failure or transition, carrying regret about "wasted" years, struggling to find identity after sport ends. Morgan played her last game feeling like she'd wasted her opportunity to live out her dreams. She wrote this book so the athletes who come after her don't have to feel that way.

The fact that I was there calling her last game and had no idea what she was going through—that's the whole point. Athletes are incredibly good at hiding this. Coaches, parents, broadcasters, teammates—we're all missing it because we're looking at the wrong things. We see the calm interview before the game. We see the hit up the middle. We don't see the numbness, the disconnection, the years of slowly losing yourself while trying to meet everyone else's expectations.

Morgan's legacy won't just be about teaching athletes how to field a ground ball or make a throw on the run to first base. It's about helping them stay whole while competing. It's about giving them the words and tools to handle the hard stuff before it becomes life-altering. It's about making sure they can look back on their college careers and feel proud instead of relieved that the pressure is finally over.

I'm grateful Morgan wrote this book. I'm grateful she was willing to share the messy truth about what she went through. And I'm grateful the next generation of athletes will have something I didn't have when I was a softball player at Texas A&M—the ability to recognize what's happening and ask for help before they're done playing, feeling like it all meant nothing.

Read this book. Whether you're an athlete, a parent, or a coach—read it. Morgan earned every word.

— *Amanda Scarborough*
ESPN Softball Analyst and 2-time DI All-American softball player

CONTENTS

INTRODUCTION

I grabbed my bat and waited at the entrance of the dugout, watching the Missouri infielders take their between-inning ground balls. It was the top of the 7th inning, and I was set to be the third hitter. This would be my last collegiate at-bat, and I was feeling... nothing. Not nerves. Not excitement. Not even sadness. Just numb.

After the second out, it felt like I was watching myself walk toward the plate. I took the sign from Coach Tarr and waved my bat back and forth across the strike zone like I always did. I'd spent the whole year preparing myself for what I'd feel in this moment—what it would be for me: a sad ending, the traditional scene I'd been a part of for teammates before me, a recognition of all the years I'd spent working, one with hugs and even tears.

But it wasn't that.

As I stood there, waiting for the pitch, I didn't feel anything. The anticipation of this final at-bat had been built up too much, and now I felt disconnected and knew the people watching didn't care much, either.

As the first pitch went by—ball one—my eyes wandered to the dugout. A teammate who didn't play was crying. I looked up at the scoreboard. Still losing. I scanned the stands for my mom—the only family member who'd come.

I wasn't thinking about the game. I wasn't present in my own ending.

This wasn't a movie where I was the main character. This was just... over.

Back in the box, I was mad that I couldn't just have this one at-bat for myself. I was determined to focus on the next pitch. I swung and muscled the ball off my hands. It wasn't pretty, but it ended up going up the middle, and I actually got a hit. At least I wasn't our last out.

Standing on first, I looked up above the first base dugout, and there was my mom with her camera, crying. The sight of her was the only thing that made me feel a fraction of the emotion I thought I would. I was hoping to feel proud in this moment, but I felt insignificant—like my mom was looking down on someone who could have done so much more with her time at Washington, and been so much more as an athlete and as a person.

Vic was the next hitter. As I took my lead and saw her bat hit the ball, I knew I had to try to beat the play—it was coming right at me. The second baseman got it before I could get by.

She ran me down and tagged me hard in the gut.

Career over.

And, in that moment, I felt like my career had amounted to absolutely nothing.

Four years earlier, I was so excited to play college softball. I'd dreamed about how I'd play—the emotion I thought I'd play with, the pride, the accomplishment. Instead, I had turned off all my feelings just to survive the pressure, the expectations, and a relationship that convinced me my own experience didn't matter.

I knew something was very wrong and had been for a while.

Standing on that field in Missouri, I finally understood: I'd robbed myself of my own career. Not because of my stats or the losses, but because I'd spent so much time hiding, performing, and seeking everyone else's approval that I'd forgotten how to actually be present.

I don't want any other athlete to feel that way after their last out.

My name is Morgan Stuart. I played softball at the University of Washington from 2008 to 2011.

This book isn't about softball. It isn't just about me. It's about the college experience no one tells you about. It's my hope that my stories will help you have a better experience than I did.

It's about what happens when you tie your entire identity to being good at something and then spend four years learning that being good isn't enough. It's about the weight gain nobody talks about, the isolation that makes everything worse, the moments that shake your sense of safety, and the day you realize you've been acting "fine" for so long that you forgot how to actually feel anything.

College is an amazing opportunity to grow. It's a place where high-level athletes can gain an upper hand in the "real world" because they know the power of the process, hard work, and learning from failure.

But there's a big risk when the stakes are this high: you can spend four years so focused on not failing that you forget to actually experience your life.

Every college athlete I know has had moments where they question everything. The sports change—softball, basketball, swimming, soccer, track—but the psychological impact stays the same. We all pretend it's "part of the experience" instead of acknowledging that some of this is genuinely hard, needs to be named, and can be prepared for. Some athletes feel these moments and can move forward; others stay stuck. Which one will you be?

High school athletes heading to college have no roadmap, no real insight into what's coming, so it's been hard to know how prepared they truly are.

That's part of the excitement, part of "growing up," but also a big reason why the college experience can mean so many different things. A *lot* of college players compete hesitantly, distracted by insecurity, fear of failing, or judgment. So many finish their careers having to rediscover who they are, with no idea what to do after their sport ends.

I'm tired of watching athletes go through the same things I went through in silence.

I want the athletes who come after me to recognize the signs earlier, reach out sooner, and understand their worth faster. I want them to know that emotions are normal, not a personal failure. I want them to know that college doesn't have to be a four-year exercise in merely trying to hang on; it's their time to go for it full speed and then make adjustments if needed.

These are the words I wish I'd had—the messy, real stories about what it's actually like.

I know I won't prevent athletes from struggling, and I don't want to. The struggles are essential steps in becoming who they're meant to be. Instead, my goal is to help them struggle better.

A few years back, I saw a video from former WNBA player, Olympic gold medalist, and current coach at Duke, Kara Lawson, that perfectly displays this point. She recalls a conversation she had with a player: "One of the things we talked about was how we all wait in life for things to get easier. Think in your own life if you've waited for something to get easier [...] 'I've just got to get through my junior year of high school and then the classes are gonna get easier.' [...] It's what we do: we wait for stuff to get easier. It will never get easier. What happens is you handle hard better."

This is growth. It's not circumstantial. You aren't better because the pressure lets up. You're better because you've learned how to adjust, how to react in a healthier way. You're stronger because the tough times unlocked that inside of you. And everyone deserves to give themselves the best chance of doing just that.

CHAPTER 1
PREPARING FOR COLLEGE

MY PLAYER STAT SHEET *At Riverside Poly High School*
• A four-year starter at Riverside Poly
• In each of her final two seasons named the Ivy League MVP, first-team all-county and first-team all-state
• Led her team to three consecutive league championships (2004–2006) and the 2004 CIF Championship
• A two-time team captain
• Named a Scholar-Athlete in each of her four seasons
• Played summer ball for the OC Batbusters under Doug Myers and the Corona Angels under Marty Tyson.[1]

1 University of Washington Athletics, "Morgan Stuart — Softball," GoHuskies, https://gohuskies.com/sports/softball/roster/stuart-morgan/2791

DON'T LET THE FUTURE TAKE YOU AWAY FROM "NOW"

I was fifteen years old the first time a college coach mentioned I had "potential" and asked my travel coach how tall my dad was.

That's when I realized: they weren't just recruiting who I was. They were betting on who I'd become. My dad was 6'5", drafted by the Dolphins as an offensive lineman. I'd inherited his big hands, strength... but I wasn't a natural "hitter." Growing up, at hitting lessons, I'd heard: "Once this bat catches up to the rest of your game..."

The hitting wasn't there yet. And every time someone said "potential," I heard: *not ready*. I kept thinking I had more time before I'd be judged, more time to figure it out.

But that was the mistake. Being recruited means you're already being judged. There is no "not yet"—the evaluation is happening whether you feel ready or not.

I spent years waiting for permission to be good enough, waiting to feel ready. But ready wasn't something I was going to feel. It was something I had to decide I was—and keep working anyway.

Many high school athletes feel this way—the pressure to perform for a future that feels completely out of their control. I was scared knowing my future was at least a little out of my hands. But here's what I learned: some things *are* in your control.

TAKE CONTROL

When everything *feels* out of your control, here's what actually *is* in your control:

Getting clear on the rules: Know when and how you should be contacting coaches and when they should be contacting you. The rules change every year, so even your coaches might not be 100 percent up to date. The website ncsasports.org has amazing resources.

Always playing like someone is watching: When you're always "on," you never have to "turn it on" and play bigger than what you've practiced. A lot of nerves come from putting unnecessary pressure on performing when coaches are watching.

Before you can contact coaches, you might wonder: What level am I at? How do I compare? A recurring theme throughout recruiting is the feeling of being judged—waiting for someone else to decide if you're good enough.

At the start of my process, I certainly felt that weight. But one perspective that eventually helped me was realizing that schools also needed to meet my standards. The fit had to go both ways.

Beyond the practical steps above, the recruiting process will test you emotionally with things that *feel* out of your control. Here are the two lessons that helped me navigate this time.

LESSON ONE: IT WILL WORK OUT

Many young athletes I work with in Anaheim are anxious because they see friends announcing commitments to big Division I schools on social media. They ask me constantly: "What do I need to work on? Why haven't I been recruited yet?"

Here's what I tell them: You don't need to follow everyone else's timeline. Your process is your own, and it will work out as long as you don't give up.

The recruiting process was different for me than it is now. I received letters in the mail from schools like Washington, Michigan, Virginia, Arizona, Arizona State, and more. I was determined to go Division I, ideally in the Pac-10 and close to home. This emotionally charged situation made things incredibly stressful. It felt like securing a scholarship was the only validation of all the years I'd spent playing travel ball and all the money my parents had invested. I thought that if I didn't get a scholarship, it would mean I wasn't good enough—that I hadn't measured up.

In today's age of social media, this perspective can be particularly damaging. The focus should be on having fun and trusting the process. Even as a kid, while I knew that my way of thinking about my worth was misguided, I couldn't help but feel that way. It seemed so black and white: if I didn't get the scholarship, I would be a failure.

My goal now is to help young athletes broaden their perspectives and move beyond that extreme thinking. So many factors influence whether you receive a Division I offer from a school like Florida or UCLA. If a school doesn't need a player in your position or if they don't have your major, they won't offer you a scholarship. It's crucial to consider the bigger picture.

When I say, "It will work out," I mean that it's not over until you decide to give up. There are plenty of options available. Choosing a Division II school or a community college might initially feel disappointing, as if you haven't achieved your goal. However, I've learned from coaching many girls, and from my own experiences, that numerous paths can lead to fulfilling outcomes, whether that's enjoying a great college experience, playing for Team USA, or going professional in softball. Many top athletes in the sport come from varied backgrounds and college experiences.

Please remember: your recruiting journey is personal, not pass/fail.

A few years ago, an athlete whom I will call Teressa (I won't use her real name here) approached me after a lesson and asked, "What do I need to work on now?" Each lesson we did with her group was an hour long. Throughout the lesson, each player got advice, cues, and adjustments from various coaches, and drills they could do at home. Every single lesson, despite all the feedback she got, she would come up and ask, "What can I get better at? What do I need to work on now?" I would ask the question back to her and ask her to explain what she thought about her process and performance in the lesson. Did she not understand the adjustments we had gone over in the last hour?

However, after a few weeks of this, I noticed how she looked me in the eye when she spoke, but then quickly looked away when I started speaking. Her shoulders would slump, and she would fidget with her glove. I suspected there was a deeper reason she continued to ask me. It wasn't just her performance she was worried about... it was how colleges would perceive her or grade that performance against what they wanted.

What she really meant was, *Why haven't they picked me yet? What am I doing wrong? Am I good enough? Do they see me as an asset?*

These questions were valid, especially since she wasn't receiving the offers she hoped for. However, they also reflected a victim mentality. When someone asks, "Why me?" they may overlook the fact that their journey is far from over. Just because some athletes had secured offers, it didn't mean it was too late for her. This mindset could have held her back from considering potential opportunities ahead.

What she really needed to hear: your timeline is your own. The schools you want might have already filled spots, but that doesn't mean your journey is over. To help players like her shift this perspective and embrace the recruiting process as a unique journey, I have a few pieces of advice:

1. **Take Responsibility for Your Process:** Don't let your parents complete the questionnaires or compose emails for you. Take control and make the communications your own. Stand out by researching the schools you're interested in and asking thoughtful questions in your emails. You may not always receive responses, but if you're asking them to invest in you by offering a scholarship, it's essential to demonstrate that you're also willing to invest your time and effort.

2. **Understand What You Want During Visits:** Before visiting schools, determine what you're looking for and why. Many athletes express a desire to play Division I, but the reasoning often stops at wanting to be on TV or win a national championship. It's important to recognize that attending a Division I school often means prioritizing your sport above academics and other aspects of life—essentially, it becomes your job. If this isn't the lifestyle you want, consider that carefully.

Also, think about the distance of the school from your hometown. Do you want your parents at every game, or would you prefer distance? Consider the type of city you want to live in. Would you be comfortable there if you got injured or could no longer play? These adult decisions can be overlooked when the focus is solely on securing a spot at a prestigious Division I program.

3. **Own Your Choices:** The choice is ultimately yours. Many athletes forget that, especially since they don't think their options are equivalent. For example, if they get an offer from one DI

school and two DII schools, they might not consider the DII schools as much based on the experience they think they want out of college: big football games, the name of a big school across their chest while playing, the opportunity to play for a championship.

However, when looking at your options of what to do after high school, you have more choices than you think. Everyone is on their own time.

When relating my experience with choosing (being recruited), I normally keep it simple and just tell the story of my choice between Washington and Arizona because that was ultimately what my choice came down to. But there was a whole process before I got to that point. The two schools were very different, but I was able to understand my reasons because of the process I had gone through before then.

When I first started thinking about the schools I would love to go to, I immediately thought about Texas because that's where my dad played. I followed the Longhorns football team and had seen players like Cat Osterman and Megan Willis play for the softball team. I saw myself living in Austin and visiting the same places my parents had when they were just meeting. I had a list of about twenty-five schools, and I sent them typed letters and emails describing why I wanted to learn more about them and what about their programs I liked. Texas was the first letter I sent out.

As I waited to hear back, I did not fully understand the recruiting windows and rules. I would be at exposure tournaments, see the coaches around the backstops, and try not to pay attention or get let down when I didn't see that Longhorn logo on one of the hats watching.

I started getting brochures in the mail. Michigan, Virginia, Washington, Cal Berkeley. None were written directly to me; these were letters with questionnaires attached. I would answer them one by one and send them back. One day, I came home from school and saw a letter addressed to me from the Texas Athletic Department. I couldn't open it fast enough.

"Dear Morgan,

Thank you for your interest in the Texas Softball Program.
Unfortunately, we have completed our 2006 recruiting class.
Good luck in your process.

Hook 'em,
Connie Clark"

The hope drained from my body the second I read the word *"unfortunately."* Not only did they not want me, but the fact that they wrote "2006 recruiting class" told me they had no idea who I was, as I was in the 2007 graduating class.

As a kid, I had no idea how many players the university was looking at around the country. I had also been told I would have a hard time hitting DI pitching in college, so I took this letter as a clue that I just wasn't good enough. It was the first letter I got that actually addressed me personally, and with Texas at the top of my list, I started to think I would need to settle for a school that I didn't really know.

The recruiting process was something I knew I couldn't control, and the only thing I knew I needed to do was hit. When I got a new hitting coach and started gaining confidence, I focused more on my hitting than on the letters I received.

The summer after my sophomore year, coaches were stacked on coaches at Nationals in South Dakota. I had gotten used to seeing coaches at games now, but this was another level.

After my high school season, where I had more success than ever, I was ready to play in front of anyone. I was the starting shortstop, I had some great at-bats, and we won the 16U National Championship that summer.

A couple of weeks after Nationals, I got two letters that lit me up and made me feel so seen. One was from Washington Coach Eve Gaw, and one was from Arizona Coach Larry Ray. They had both been faces in the crowd at the South Dakota Nationals. Coach Ray wrote about how impressive it was that I had waited on a changeup for an impactful hit during the tournament. Coach Gaw talked about how she could see me playing shortstop for the Huskies. I knew I wanted to go on trips to see these two schools after that.

The visits to each school taught me everything I needed to know about fit.

MY TRIP TO WASHINGTON

Everything that could go right did. It was sunny. The football team beat UCLA. I was nervous about spending time with other recruits and players on the current Washington team because I was shy in general, but I felt like they welcomed me and were warm and generous with their time. I remember thinking the brick buildings on campus, along with the trees and colors, were so pretty in September.

I didn't know too much about the Washington softball team or about the coaching staff. Growing up, I only really paid attention to the fact that UCLA and Arizona were dominant, that Texas had been up there... but not too much else. When they offered me a full-ride scholarship and I had that offer on the table, it made the experience everything I had ever hoped for.

MY TRIP TO ARIZONA

I got there and was underwhelmed by the campus.

Compared to Washington, the buildings were just buildings. It was hot, with almost no shade. I saw a player passing by as she was going to work out on her own, and... she was nice, but I was just a random person to her. This visit felt different immediately. At Washington, the players knew who I was and had been prepared to take me around campus and explore. Here, it was more about my meeting with Larry Ray and Mike Candrea. I couldn't believe I would get to sit in Coach Candrea's office—the Team USA head coach in the flesh.

I was led into the office and looked around at all the USA gear and National Championship trophies. It was surreal to think about playing for a coach who had been so successful. Coach Candrea explained that they really liked how I played—that Coach Ray had told him about South Dakota. They saw me as a third baseman for their team, and they could offer me a 95 percent scholarship.

MY DECISION

I had other letters expressing interest and went on another trip to Arizona State, but it was clear to me that my real choice was between Washington and Arizona. Here are the things I considered. I'm not sure if I would come to the same conclusions about each point now, but these were my real thoughts:

I grew up playing shortstop—it was my comfort and my pride. Arizona wanted me at third base. Washington wanted me at shortstop. In my mind, this meant Washington wanted me for who I already was.

Arizona offered me 95 percent. Washington offered 100 percent—another signal they were investing more in me.

The city of Seattle was exciting, with lots going on. I loved the campus and the greenery there. Tucson felt black and white comparatively.

Lastly, the people. I was made to feel so welcome at Washington. The one player I met at Arizona didn't seem to know who I was.

Twelve-year-old me would have bet on Arizona—all those championships, Mike Candrea, the legacy. But I chose Washington because I wanted to be part of building something. Being on their *first* National Championship team became my goal.

The choice wasn't easy, but I realized that, at some point, we can't dwell on the "what ifs." No matter which path you choose, you'll encounter challenges, hurdles, and amazing experiences—each choice brings its own set of opportunities and obstacles.

I called each school to tell them my decision. I was so nervous to call Coach Candrea to tell him no, but I was really proud of how I handled recruiting. I filled out every form myself, researched schools, and, even though it was uncomfortable, made the phone calls I needed to.

Once you make a decision, it's important to fully commit to that path. Many young people often get caught up in whether they are making the right choice. While it's vital to consider the implications of your decision, remember that you're making it for a reason. You must believe in yourself and your choice.

LESSON TWO: BE PRESENT

Be where your feet are because time flies. As a senior in high school, I remember always looking forward—constantly thinking about what my next fall would be like, what my next training would entail, and whether I was prepared. I was fixated on the next year.

However, I received a big reality check once I got to college. My life completely changed, and I found myself wishing I could go back to cherish those moments—family dinners and the big family gatherings where we celebrated birthdays and even the smaller holidays. After moving out to college, it became uncertain if I would ever experience those moments again.

One of the greatest gifts I received during that time was a scrapbook my mom made for me. It may seem small or ordinary to receive a scrapbook for your senior year, but my mom put in countless hours of effort; it weighed close to ten pounds! Each page was dedicated to different family members: both of my aunts' families, my uncle's family, my grandparents on my mom's side, my "meemaw" and "papaw" on my dad's side, both of my brothers, my dad, and, of course, my mom, the ringleader behind it all.

Each family member wrote a letter on their designated page, sharing advice, expressing their pride in me, and reflecting on what they learned during their college experiences. My favorite letter was from my Aunt Helene, who avoided general advice and vague well-wishes. She kept it real, talked about having a designated driver for parties, and reminded me that I could always call her if I didn't want to call my parents and needed someone.

When I opened the scrapbook and started reading the letters, I cried hard—something I don't usually do. At that moment, I realized that I wouldn't have all those meaningful conversations with my family anymore in person. My life was about to change dramatically. Yes, I could pick up the phone, but I was about to leave home and live on my own, and I would miss the physical presence of my loved ones.

That scrapbook inspired me to write a book like this one. Instead of just telling athletes what to expect, I wanted to provide a more real account, addressing their nerves and the things holding them back from being their best.

As I prepared to go out of state, I realized just how important it was to treasure the time spent with family. It's essential not only to soak up the senior festivities but also to appreciate the routines and relationships that have shaped you because, before you know it, everything changes.

Looking back, significant events happened to my family during my time in school. Both of my brothers faced challenges in their sports. We were all athletes growing up. It seemed to be a part of every memory I had with them. Caleb went from playing football to trying track and field. Johnny, who seemed to be the most athletic of us all, decided he didn't want to play anything anymore.

Both of my grandpas passed away, and I wasn't there when my family received the news either time. Our two dogs at my parents' house passed, too. There were times when I was at school when it really felt like things were falling apart, and I couldn't do anything to control it.

The distance when you go away to college can affect you more than just physically; the emotional distance can take its toll, too.

I encourage each of you seniors to remain present and savor every moment. Don't focus too far into the future. You only get one senior year at home.

MY PERSONAL STAT SHEET

Based on the two lessons in this chapter, here's how I measured up personally:

1. It will work out.

> I did a good job of moving on after the Texas letter and focused on getting better as a hitter more than stressing about the recruiting letters. I would give myself an 8/10 on this lesson.

2. Be present.

> I give myself a 7/10 on this one. I am a worrier by nature, so I know I was thinking forward a lot during my senior year. I was still able to enjoy prom, senior pictures, and being part of my high school team.

CHAPTER 2
FRESHMAN YEAR

MY PLAYER STAT SHEET *2008 (As a Freshman)*
• Honorable Mention All-Pac-10
• Ranked fifth on the team with a .288 batting average while leading the Huskies in RBI (39) and tying for the team lead with seven home runs
• Started 55 of the 56 games, missing one game to an injury
• Hit her first career home run and went 2-for-3 with three RBI and a double against UMKC (Feb. 15)
• Named MVP of the Malihini Kipa Aloha Tournament after hitting .526 with a tournament-best 12 RBI and adding two doubles and two home runs
• Hit 2-for-4 with an RBI against Texas at the NCAA Regional on May 17
• Hit a solo home run in the season finale against Houston the next day.

PREPARED BUT NOT READY

I showed up to campus weighing 143 pounds with the conditioning packet completed, dorm layout already planned, and a roommate I'd already met. I kept telling myself: *At least I'm probably more prepared than some people here.*

But I still had questions spinning in my head: *Should I bring my bat bag to practice? Do I wear my cleats? When will they tell us exactly where to be and when?* I'd done everything I could to prepare, but the anxiety about all the unknowns wouldn't go away.

Reflecting on those early days, I realized that my theme for freshman year revolved around the idea that I thought I had everything figured out. As someone who is a perfectionist, I created checklists and gathered all the supplies I needed for my dorm. However, one of the biggest insights I gained was the realization that there wasn't ever just one answer that would make me feel "ready," and some questions only got answered once you got there. Just showing up was what I truly needed to do.

In hindsight, having everything scripted and perfect wasn't necessary. In high school, I had always followed a step-by-step method, but as my freshman year unfolded, I learned that it would primarily be about learning. I sincerely wish I hadn't felt overwhelmed by the pressure of not knowing everything at all times.

As I share these stories, my advice for you during your freshman year is: be ready to be thrown into the deep end and to embrace a learning mindset instead of feeling like you need to master everything before arriving on campus.

LESSON ONE: PREPARATION PUTS YOU IN A DIFFERENT CLASS

The summer before I stepped onto campus as a freshman, I was emailed a conditioning packet. This was my first assignment as a college kid, and I was going to be all over it. The packet explained that all players needed to pass a conditioning test to participate in fall team practices. I hadn't ever prepared for a test like this, but I knew that it would be the focus of the rest of my summer. It was *that* important to me not to be the one who didn't pass.

Our conditioning test consisted of a 300-yard shuttle run, broken up into 25-yard increments. While at home in Riverside, California, I marked out 25 yards in our backyard to practice. Dusty and so, so hot. I'd always raked away the rocks and weeds in the back half of our backyard for groundball reps. I had my own infield back there, with my pitchback and pop-up net.

This summer, I'd be out there running my six trips down and back just about every day—or at least every other day—to ensure I was in shape and wouldn't embarrass myself during the test.

The summer heat in Riverside averages around 95 degrees, and some days I purposely ran at noon to make my test a little harder than I knew it would be in Seattle in the fall.

I didn't know whether we would be inside or outside for the test. When I imagined running, I pictured a football field. I knew my nerves would be going, so I'd have a little extra adrenaline to help me out.

The passing times varied by position; I had to complete each shuttle in under 62 seconds. You ran two shuttles with a minute break in between. If you set a great time on the first one, you had to run the second within five seconds of that time. For example, if you completed the first in 56 seconds, you had to finish the second in no more than 61 seconds to pass.

On the day of the test, we were in the Dempsey Indoor. This had an indoor football field, complete with a track around the perimeter. The ceilings were super high, and there was always a distinct smell from the rubber beads in the turf floor.

We lined up. There were two groups of us, and I was in the first one with two of the other freshmen. As we waited for the whistle to go, my stomach turned, even though I knew I had to be more ready than half of the people on the line.

I heard the whistle and took off. From all the practice I'd had in my backyard, I knew not to start in a sprint. I went right to the pace I was used to.

Three turns down, and I felt good. I was keeping up and more.

Five turns down, and I was well ahead of the other freshmen.

When I crossed the finish line, I was at 60 seconds, and I felt good. I had prepped and was head and shoulders above the two others I had imagined would be on my level coming in.

In the end, I crushed my test and felt amazing about it. While some fellow freshmen struggled and didn't make it, witnessing others' struggles only boosted my confidence. I realized that preparation really does make a difference.

I had my steps figured out, and one important thing I learned about myself was that if I knew how to prepare, I would do it. I wanted to avoid the embarrassment of being unprepared. However, if the preparation wasn't straightforward or I wasn't sure what I needed to do to feel more mentally ready for the next challenge, I struggled.

For example, going into my freshman year, one of my biggest weaknesses was my mindset regarding facing Division I pitching. I had been told since childhood that it would be incredibly difficult for me. Not understanding how to prepare my mindset really held me back.

One of my biggest regrets from my freshman year is that I didn't approach everything like I did with my fitness test. I didn't actively seek out the knowledge I needed to feel more prepared. If I had only known that having the illusion of being "ready" could come from knowing I was putting in the work—like doing reps in the 95-degree heat in Riverside—I would have felt more confident and secure in my abilities.

If I had applied that same determination to other aspects of my college experience, like my hitting and the mental approach behind it, I would have been in a better spot moving forward.

LESSON TWO: LEARN YOUR BODY, MACROS MATTER

The fall of my freshman year was much different than my senior year in California. Once October hit, the clouds rolled in, and I learned quickly that every day, there would be at least a little rain while living in Seattle.

Other changes affected me even more. Workouts were every day. We not only needed to attend class and practice, but we also were required to sign up for study halls, tutoring, and extra workouts. I didn't have a lot of free time, but I made up for that with freedom in everything else: I lived in the dorms, with access to buffet dinners and dining hall snacks anytime I wanted. On weekends without practice, it was normal to go to parties, drink, stay out late, and generally go crazy without regard for how it would impact play.

I had always been thin and muscular growing up. I never worried about my weight and knew that I was pretty skinny when I showed up to fall practices. When I started eating more, I knew I needed it because I was working out and running around just to keep up with my schedule... but I didn't really pay attention to the type of food I was eating. I especially didn't pay attention to what I was putting in my body over the weekends, when I wasn't just fueling for workouts; I was drinking to excess and paying no attention to what was "healthy."

I clearly remember walking through the door of my house after flying home for Christmas. My mom saw me and started crying. She said, "Now I have to buy you all new jeans." She had already bought me Christmas presents. One glimpse of me, and she was shocked by my sudden weight gain.

"Macros" is short for "macronutrients." When I came to campus, I weighed 143 pounds, but by the time I returned home for Christmas, I had ballooned to 175 pounds.

This is common for athletes, especially female athletes. We often hear that we need to get bigger, stronger, and faster, but this process also changes how we perceive ourselves and our relationship with food. As athletes, we have to see our bodies as instruments. Our physical performance is our livelihood, and we need to care about how our bodies function, how certain foods affect us, and how our weight influences our mood and movements.

Ignoring these will hold you back, and it certainly held me back during my freshman year. Coming home to see my mom's reaction was deflating—I was completely unaware that I had gained over thirty pounds. I didn't know how much of it was fat and how much of it was muscle. How had this happened? Part of it stemmed from being in sweats all the time as an athlete. I'd leave for workouts at 5:30 in the morning and return at seven at night. With access to buffets and free food at training facilities, and being constantly tired from rigorous workouts, it was easy to overeat.

I remember being told I was part of the "Big Eaters Club" on my team. I wasn't given a choice, but since this came from the upperclassmen (which meant they were paying attention to me), I didn't hesitate to identify with it and act accordingly.

They explained that the players in this club needed to order an appetizer, a main dish, and, if we could, try to fit in dessert when the team ate at restaurants on the road.

At the time, I thought it was funny, maybe even a compliment. Looking back, I can see it was a way for upperclassmen to assert power, to make the freshmen prove they "belonged" by doing something that wasn't actually something we would normally do. But as a gullible freshman eager to be liked, I didn't question it. I just went with it.

I didn't think about what my body actually needed for fuel. I didn't think that I would be costing the team more money by ordering the biggest things on the menu. I loved to eat, and I thought it was an easy way to be accepted into another group.

In reality, I was ignoring what my body actually needed in order to fit in. While caring way more about what the upperclassmen thought of me, I was completely unaware of the harm I was doing to myself—or the extra cost I was putting on the team's budget.

Food wasn't the only area where I prioritized fitting in over taking care of myself.

PARTIES AND DRINKING

As a freshman, I was navigating the independence of saying "yes" or "no" to parties, staying out late, and making choices about whether to drink or not. Being on the shy side, I'm sad to say I used alcohol as a crutch at times and didn't think of the negative impact on my body. I was more concerned about being liked, fitting in, and being thought of as someone who could be fun.

At the end of the season, we were on a plane, returning from a tournament in Houston. We had regional, super-regional, and World Series postseason games. My freshman year, we were eliminated in the regionals, and that trip to Houston was part of it.

On the plane back, I happened to be sitting next to Coach Tarr, my head coach. She asked me what one aspect I thought I needed to improve for next year. I replied, "I don't know. Maybe it was my hitting?"

She then made a comment that shocked me: "Did you know there are a hundred calories in every shot of alcohol? That adds up pretty quickly, more than a second dinner by the time you go to sleep."

I was so embarrassed that she'd brought this up, but her comment opened my eyes. It made me realize that I needed to change. That wasn't who I wanted to be.

MOST PEOPLE ONLY LEARN ABOUT "MACROS" WHEN THEY ARE LOSING WEIGHT

Seeing that I had gained thirty pounds, paired with my mom's reaction, gave me a sour taste when it came to gaining weight. But gaining weight isn't always bad. In my case, with knowingly overeating and partying, it most likely wasn't the best for me. But now, with a lot of schools having ways to measure body fat percentage and lean mass, I would have known that for sure. I wish we had done more of this when I was in school—then there would have been less shame around weight and more education about body composition.

Learning about my body and understanding macros has been an ongoing process for me—not just as an athlete, but as a person. I wish I had paid more attention to my protein needs, learned about the different types of carbs, and understood how fats could improve my mood. If I had, I would have performed much better, and I regret not having that awareness while I was playing.

We had a nutritionist visit us on occasion in college, but the attitude of the nutritionist was to "eat what makes you feel good." That didn't resonate with me because eating always felt good to me, it seemed. She would present pictures of what a plate should look like, then be back the next season with the same talk. It felt like "just another talk" the team had to attend—not serious enough to change your lifestyle.

I really wish I had taken it more seriously.

After I graduated, when I didn't have a reason to be heavier to "produce power when hitting," as my strength coach had mentioned, I felt like I started over in understanding my health. I started learning more about nutrition on my own when I set out to lose body fat. I got my hormones tested, calculated my body fat percentage, and started doing cardio.

Just like anything, when you first start learning, it can be overwhelming, with all kinds of information. It took me a while to find the information that was actually relevant to me.

I got caught up in a little diet culture: I tried keto, intermittent fasting, juice fasts, gluten-free, and Whole 30. All of these were good for a few weeks, but none felt sustainable for me. I started looking at some foods as "bad," and I was constantly worried about gaining weight back after I stopped adhering to the rules of each program.

MACROS ARE A GREAT TOOL

Years passed, and my weight fluctuated with my work, the time I had to prepare meals, and the amount of attention I actually paid to what I ate. It wasn't until I decided to get a coach that I discovered macros and finally understood calorie deficits, staying consistent, and how to eat for different goals. I had always heard about friends weighing food and counting grams. It seemed like so much work.

One of the best investments I've ever made was getting a coach, because she debunked the idea of diet culture. There were no longer bad foods, just food that helped me meet my goals or not. I didn't have to be perfect, and I no longer needed to guess what would work and what wouldn't.

I discovered macros because I was at a point in my life where I wanted to lose weight, but if I had looked at my choices through the lens of macros in college, I would have, no doubt, competed in a healthier body and mind.

LESSON THREE: MAKE FRIENDS OUTSIDE OF YOUR SPORT

When I moved into the dorms, I was grouped with a soccer athlete. Initially, I was disappointed because I had teammates on the softball team whom I had known since I was around fourteen, and I would have preferred to room with one of them for comfort. However, this turned out to be a great experience. I not only became friends with my roommate but also connected with many of her teammates, including several soccer girls from my class.

I don't have a specific memory that stands out, but I do remember sitting in the dorms, not having to talk about practice or our specific sports. We could simply be ourselves—just college kids having whatever experience life threw our way, whether we were tired, hungry, or anything else. It felt great not to be judged and to be able to express ourselves freely.

College is a wonderful place to make connections and learn about yourself. Part of this growth comes from interacting with a variety of people. If we only spend time with teammates or those who are just like us, we limit our ability to expand our horizons and discover more about the world beyond our immediate circle.

One piece of advice I would offer is to make friends outside of your sport. If you play volleyball, consider befriending soccer players or athletes from other sports. You'll gain a fresh perspective and a new set of friends. I also challenge you to connect with non-athlete classmates—it offers a completely different experience compared to the athlete lifestyle.

Looking back at my freshman year stats now—Honorable Mention All-Pac-10, leading my team in RBIs, playing in every game except one—I realize I had a significant impact. But at the time, I didn't see it. I was too focused on whether I was measuring up and who I was off the field.

Transitioning from high school, where my schedule was dictated for me, to college, where I had complete freedom and no curfews, was a bigger adjustment than I anticipated. I found myself more distracted than prepared.

I wish I had been more grounded in who I was and clearer about my goals—for preparation, nutrition, and making connections. Being firmer in my intentions and standards would have kept me on a path of learning and growth, rather than shrinking back to just fit in.

MY PERSONAL STAT SHEET

Based on the three lessons in this chapter, here's how I measured up personally:

1. Preparation puts you in a different class.

In my ability to prepare for my conditioning test: 10/10. I was ready, and I knew it.

In school, mechanics on the softball field: I'd give myself an 8/10 preparation score.

In mindset: my ability to be solid in who I was and what I let affect me: 5/10.

2. Learn your body. Macros matter.

3/10. Growing up, my mom made a lot of our meals. We didn't drink soda. We did know what proteins, carbs, and fats were, but I didn't continue learning about what would be best for me when I had the freedom to choose. I made things exponentially worse by including alcohol as much as I did. Highly *do not* recommend.

3. Make friends outside of your sport.

6/10. I did not go out of my way to make friends, but I am grateful my dorm environment brought the right people into my life.

CHAPTER 3
SOPHOMORE YEAR

MY PLAYER STAT SHEET

2009 (Sophomore)

- Named Honorable Mention All-Pac-10 and was also named to the Women's College World Series All-Tournament team
- First-Team Academic All-Pac-10 and was also given the UW's Provost Academic Excellence Award
- Named an Arthur Ashe Jr. Sports Scholar with her 3.48 GPA
- Set a Women's College World Series record with four doubles and tied a record by recording five hits in a single game
- Batted .476 in the six games, with a World Series-high 10 hits in 21 at-bats
- Her 10 postseason RBI gave her 37 for the season to take over the team lead
- One of two Huskies to start all 63 games, starting 27 at short and 36 at third base.

MY BEST YEAR

Sophomore year was the best of all of them—not just statistically, but in how I felt about myself and how safe I felt on my team. I use the word "protected" because I didn't have high expectations of myself. We had nine seniors that season, which took the pressure off me.

Having a year of experience gave me confidence. I knew what was coming: the fall season, training, conference play, postseason. I felt more prepared than I'd ever feel again.

LESSON ONE: THERE ARE NO GUARANTEES IN SPORTS

The story that comes to mind starts with what I expected with my commitment to Washington. The coaches at the time told me that they wanted me as their starting shortstop. I took that as: I would be the starting shortstop. As a high school student transitioning to college, that was incredibly reassuring. They wanted me to occupy that crucial position, and during my recruiting trip, they even had me practice at shortstop. This was a major factor in my decision to commit to the school.

However, once I got on campus and into the season, reality set in. Though the team and coaching staff had high hopes for me, and I did, too, I took reps behind Ashley Charters—and began to feel this more than I was told: there are no guarantees in sports. Injuries can occur, team dynamics can change, personal performance can fluctuate, and the matchups against opponents can vary day to day.

Going into freshman year, I expected to play shortstop. Let me clarify: I didn't want it handed to me, but based on my recruiting visit and talks with coaches, I expected the spot to be open. Looking back, I was naïve. I didn't understand that teams need more than one shortstop, and that relying on an unproven freshman is risky.

When I got to campus in 2008, Ashley Charters was the starting shortstop. It was her senior season. She was excellent. A very different player than I was... left-handed, fast, light on her feet. Charters was a multi-time All-American who went on to play professionally and for Team USA. She was one of my favorite teammates ever.

That fall, she and I would switch off at shortstop. I hoped to learn from her, but I didn't think I'd be playing over her.

Then she had the option to undergo surgery for an injury. If she'd chosen to play through the pain, that position wouldn't have been open to me. I was fortunate it worked out, but it taught me: even when you're told one thing, there are no guarantees.

This serves as a reality check for anyone going through the recruiting process or currently experiencing college athletics. It's crucial to weigh all the various factors. Even if you're not starting or things aren't going as planned, many factors can affect the situation. If you're feeling disappointed about things not going ideally or as previously laid out, it's often not solely your fault. Rarely does a singular event lead to a specific outcome.

Another example I think about involves my freshman class, which started with five of us: me, Jace, Aleah, Ashley, and Courtney. This often happens—the group you enter college with is rarely the same by the time you graduate. Although we began as a standout freshman class, only two of us graduated from Washington after completing our entire college experience there.

I reflect on this often because recruiters and travel ball coaches often portray a black-and-white picture. In reality, no one can predict the experience you will have. Too many choices are involved.

Many factors can influence our experiences, and things can shift very quickly. Our greatest asset during our college experience is the ability to adjust. Instead of depending on a picture painted for us about desired outcomes, when the moment comes and it doesn't look like we thought, we do our best to move forward and adjust instead of getting stuck comparing to the original picture.

LESSON TWO: BE A GOOD TEAMMATE

Growing up, I was always proud to be the shortstop. If you talk to any baseball or softball player, they'll tell you that shortstop is often played by one of the best athletes on the team—typically a strong fielder and a leader, someone the team can look up to.

I liked being seen this way as a player. In my freshman year, I was the starting shortstop, a distinction I partially earned and partially owed to Charters's redshirting. Heading into my sophomore year, I started the fall season in the same position. However, halfway through the conference play, Jenn Salling transferred from Oregon to Washington and joined our team.

Jenn had previously played for Team Canada and was an All-American and an Olympian. I knew she was an amazing player and that the conversation was coming.

Coach Tarr brought me into her office and said, “Hey, we’re thinking about putting Jenn at shortstop and moving you to third base. How do you feel about that?”

My response was easy because I wanted to play: “Whatever the team needs.”

But in the moment, I remember thinking, *Well, maybe I can beat her out.* Others in the same position might have gotten stuck on the fact that this wasn’t “fair.”

I talk a lot about what I regret about my playing experience or things I would have changed, but this is something that I am proud of and what makes me who I am. This was one of the coolest things I contributed to in that championship team: we were an amazing left side, and I think I became a better third baseman than I was a shortstop because I couldn’t have cared less about what was fair.

Fairness has no place in competitive sports.

I told anyone who asked me how great Jenn was (because she was —a freak of nature on both sides of the ball) and that this was the right call because she was a better shortstop than me... and I didn't just say that because it was better for the team—I said that because it was the truth. Beyond the timing, beyond the fact it was “my spot” before that moment... the only thing that mattered to me (mattered in general) was the belief that the best combination of players should be on the field.

Players get too caught up in “What did I do wrong, Coach?” The real question we should ask ourselves is, *Am I the* ***best*** *option for the job?*

Each of my teammates worked hard like me; we all had different strengths, and, thankfully, it wasn't my job to worry about making the lineup.

A lot of mindset is about believing in yourself. Another big part is understanding how to thrive in team sports: it's not personal; it's not about you. Your responsibility as a player is to work on being your best wherever you are. Everything else is just noise.

My response is something I take great pride in—among many regrets I have about my college experience, this is not one of them.

I said, " I want to do whatever is best for the team."

As a result of that choice, I had some incredible experiences at third base. By being open to this change, I was able to train one-on-one with Coach Tarr, who had played third base herself when she was a player at Washington. This mentorship was an invaluable experience that I wouldn't have received if I had reacted negatively to the position change.

I also developed a great relationship with Jenn, who was a bit nervous about joining the team since she didn't know how everyone would accept her. Because my reaction was one of support, we quickly established a friendship based on shared values—we both wanted to win. During our sophomore year, we started the season ranked 13th, but with Jenn on the team and a strong infield, including our outstanding pitcher Danielle, we knew we had what it took to go far in the postseason and potentially win the championship.

This lesson about being a good teammate is crucial because many players become consumed with their personal performance, struggles during the season, and the distractions of college life. College is a time of intense personal growth, and feeling overwhelmed can taint the experience. By focusing on being a good teammate, we concentrate on what truly matters—not just in winning games, but in navigating life as a whole. We won't go through life alone; how we impact those around us plays a much more significant role in our futures than how we performed in a single game or our final batting averages.

Among all my experiences, this moment stands out as one of my proudest achievements as a teammate.

The last point I want to make is about the difference between being supportive when everything is going your way versus when someone "takes your position." I believe there's a significant difference in the internal conversation you have during those times. If you're focused on what's best for the team, it's rare that you'll become fixated on the position being yours.

Even though I took great pride in being a shortstop and embodied certain characteristics associated with that position, those traits didn't take precedence over my need to be a good teammate. It's not that you can't learn this mindset, but if it's not naturally part of you, it's something you need to grasp very quickly, especially if you're involved in a team sport.

If you participate in individual sports like golf or tennis, your primary focus might not be the team. However, life itself is a team sport. In any context, whether you're part of a family unit, a daughter, a sister, a wife, a teammate, or part of your graduating class, you are always part of a group.

If you're someone who struggles to prioritize what's best for everyone while still striving to be your best self, that can lead you down a difficult path.

LESSON THREE: WHEN YOU'RE NOT THE STAR, CONTRIBUTE IN OTHER WAYS

In softball, the regular season (conference play) is followed by a three-weekend postseason, with the final round lasting about a week: regionals, super regionals, and the World Series.

Sixty-four teams qualify for regionals, competing at sixteen host sites with four teams each. Only sixteen teams advance to super regionals at eight sites. After that weekend, just eight teams remain nationally. In 2008, we didn't make it out of regionals. In 2009, we reached the World Series.

It felt like a dream to reach the World Series. During our Super Regional weekend at Georgia Tech, I was hitting balls off the wall. I'd historically been an inconsistent hitter, but that weekend was different—I was seeing the ball consistently. It felt like I had reached that "potential" my coaches had always hoped for.

When we got to the World Series, I was feeling great. I had the best start to a tournament I had ever experienced. The TV cameras were on, my parents were in the stands, and everything was clicking. I felt incredibly present; I can even remember the distinctive smell of the dirt at the field—it reminded me of the smell of crayons when you open the box. I always had a pregame snack of peanut butter pretzels as I walked up to the dugout.

I felt really comfortable, which surprised me because I had always been a bit nervous, anxious, and quiet throughout my life as an athlete. I never truly believed in myself when the spotlight was on me. However, during this championship series, everything felt completely different. This newfound confidence had been building throughout the games leading up to the championship.

In the tournament's first four games, I managed at least one hit per game. At one point, I was even leading the entire tournament in batting average, doubles, and hits, which was pretty incredible. When we made it to the championship series, the format was a bracket-style best of three, meaning it was just us and one other team left—either we or they would take first place.

Walking into the championship series, I was already feeling confident from my previous performance. However, in my first couple of at-bats during the game, I struck out and made some poor outs. It was evident that the other team had studied my film; they figured they could beat me with change-ups. I faced three, four, even five change-ups in a row, and I couldn't make any adjustments.

Here's where the important lesson comes in: I was in such a resilient mental space that when I walked back to the dugout after striking out, I wasn't upset at all. I had performed well in previous games, and with nine seniors on the team, I didn't feel the pressure of having to score all the runs or get all the hits.

I've never been a player who focused on myself, but at that moment, I responded to failure in a healthy way. I realized that if I couldn't be the one to get the hit, I could still contribute positively by giving good energy, not missing high-fives as I returned to the dugout, maintaining eye contact, and keeping up the offense. It wasn't about me.

I can recall times in my career, particularly my junior year, which I would describe as my worst, when I made it all about me. I was so upset with myself for not coming through that it affected my ability to be a good teammate or to respond positively to setbacks. I struggled to forget about what had just happened and move on.

Now, let me share a celebration story that ties into this lesson. In 2009, I had a double in one of the championship series games. In my last at-bat, with either the bases loaded or a runner on third, they had figured out how to pitch to me. I ended up hitting a slow dribbler back to the pitcher, who bobbled it while trying to get an out. The runner came around to score, and that was the winning run. We won the championship game three to two, largely because I kept swinging, even though it wasn't a perfect hit—just an error. I scored the winning run, and it was one of the happiest moments I'd ever had playing.

THE CELEBRATION CONTINUED

After the game, we were unsure how to celebrate. We'd never won a championship before.

We went back to the hotel, had dinner with our parents, just like after every game. Then we got an announcement: "We're all going out on the bus. Be downstairs in ten minutes." It suddenly hit me that the freshmen and sophomores probably wouldn't be invited since we were underage.

I spent time with my parents, but because they thought I was going on the bus, they left quickly. I went back to my room and quickly changed in case the plan turned out we actually *wouldn't* be going to bars... I hopped out of my hotel room and got down the elevator with a light jog out to where the bus had been parked. A senior teammate was texting me to *"Hurry!"*

I made it outside just in time to see the bus pull away. *Why hadn't they waited to at least let us know the plan?* My night turned immediately sad... thinking about how this huge accomplishment had finally happened, yet I felt disconnected.

My last memory of that hotel room after we won the championship was sitting by myself, re-watching the World Series game alone. It was a strange ending to the celebration.

One aspect that really hit me hard was that most of the people on the bus were seniors, and I realized I would never play with them again. With their departure, I suddenly felt more expectations and pressure on my shoulders. I think that contributed to the self-doubt that began to brew as we flew back home to Washington for more celebration and to reset for the next season. With the abrupt ending to the championship night, I felt everything had changed in a second.

Sophomore year was the best it would ever be. I just didn't know it yet.

The pressure I'd avoided with nine seniors carrying the load was about to land squarely on my shoulders.

MY PERSONAL STAT SHEET

1. There are no guarantees.

> 9/10. I didn't expect anything to be given to me. Sometimes, I think I was a little too good at this skill because if I had "expected" to be an All-American instead of being realistic all the time, maybe I would have achieved more excellence.

2. Be a good teammate.

> 7/10. Even though the story I told about Jenn was an example of me being a good teammate, this was a year when times were good. My biggest regret is being a not-so-

great teammate in my tougher times, when it wasn't so easy.

3. When you're not the star, try to contribute in other ways.

7/10 for my sophomore year... 5/10 for an average of my career. I always felt like I could be consistent on defense when my hitting wasn't working, but if this is a score for my whole career, my mindset held me back from contributing more because I completely shut down at times.

CHAPTER 4
JUNIOR YEAR

MY PLAYER STAT SHEET *2010 (Junior)*
• Appeared and started in all 59 games
• Batted .227, collecting 35 hits in 154 at-bats with three home runs, six doubles, and 14 RBIs
• In Husky year-by-year record book and tied for fourth in Husky individual season record book for hit by pitch (11)
• First-Team Academic All-Pac-10 for the second-straight year.

EXPECTATIONS AND ISOLATION

Junior year is why I do this work.

The reason I'm so passionate about helping young athletes is rooted in 2010. I wouldn't say I regret the whole year—it significantly shaped who I am today. But knowing that my twelve-year-old self would have wanted a different experience makes me sad. What I lived through this year taught me about mental health, emotions, and the importance of asking for help.

We all need to go through struggles. But I wish I'd struggled better.

As I entered junior year, I felt an unprecedented weight on my shoulders. Freshman year, I had some pressure, but it wasn't intense. No one really knew who I was. Sophomore year was lighter—I understood my responsibilities, and we had nine seniors to carry the load.

Junior year was different. Those nine seniors had graduated. The expectations fell heavily on me. I had proven myself to be a strong hitter and a leader, and I felt the pressure to continue being that clutch player. If I didn't meet those expectations, I was afraid I wouldn't live up to what everyone imagined I could be. No older upperclassman was there to help me if I faltered.

LESSON ONE: PROCESSING EMOTIONS ALONE MAGNIFIES EVERYTHING

The fall season in college softball spans from late August through November, when you are getting acclimated to new teammates, learning plays, and engaging in intensive strength workouts. This is when you establish a foundation for the season ahead.

During our fall, we had a home tournament where our crowd was excited, especially because we were the returning national champions. Danielle, our pitcher, was back, and she had been phenomenal the previous year. As a result, we were ranked number one going into the season. When the preseason All-American list was released and my name appeared on it for the first time, it only added to the weight of my expectations.

Unfortunately, I didn't handle this newfound pressure well. Throughout the fall, I struggled to hit, which made me feel like I wasn't contributing. After the season, I went home and attempted to practice with my coach, but I didn't improve.

As we entered conference play, I felt hesitant in the batter's box, overwhelmed by the worst version of me talking in my head. You've probably been in this place and know: It's incredibly challenging to adopt a positive mindset when you're already in a bad place.

I didn't want to be "fake positive" to try to pull myself out of the funk, which left me unsure of what else to do aside from practicing more or watching more videos. My days became a routine where I'd wake up unhappy because I had performed poorly the day before, whether in practice or during a game. I would arrive at the field early and do my warm-up reps, and with every rep, I couldn't help but think about my previous mistakes and what I had done wrong.

I never really motivated myself or thought neutrally about the situation. A neutral mindset would have been, *Okay, what happened yesterday doesn't affect today*. Instead, I'd think, *That happened yesterday, so now people are expecting me to either continue performing poorly or finally break out of my slump.* Either way, I was not in a good place.

I recognized that my self-talk was detrimental.

During early reps and while watching videos of my performance, I focused on my mistakes and was overly critical about what I should be doing better. I'd say things in my head like, *I just suck. Why am I even in the lineup?*

I would play my game, underperform (not get a hit or focus on mistakes), then drive home and shut myself in my room so my mood wouldn't bleed onto everyone else.

Part of me wanted to talk about it, to let it all out and reset, but I also didn't want to come off as needy, a burden, or weak to my friends and teammates.

I thought, *This is my fault. I should be able to fix it. Just change my mind. Focus on being grateful, focus on what I did right.*

All good tactics... but my problem was that I had already built up too much negativity, and my habits largely allowed for the hurtful self-talk to outweigh any positive talk I could muster up.

I needed a change, help, or a way to be held accountable for what I was saying to myself, but I didn't seek those out. I did what came naturally: I bundled up in my bedroom (a converted basement), alone with my thoughts to try to sort them out myself while I scrapbooked, journaled, or tuned my feelings out with *Grey's Anatomy*.

I found myself constantly watching reruns of the same show. Out of everything I tried, it was one of the only things that gave me some comfort. I had all the seasons on DVD and would just sit there, especially in Seattle's fall (when it gets increasingly rainy, dark, and cloudy), cycling through episodes and full seasons.

Mental health and the mental game are completely different things. I want to make this clear, as well as the fact that I am *not* a mental health professional in any way.

But this time in my life made me see that the line between the two can be very thin if we don't secure our foundation of mental wellness before anything else.

My sense of self-worth and my ability to feel safe and secure with myself were threatened when I couldn't let myself off the hook and reset. I didn't know who I was when I wasn't successful. I didn't let anyone else know me either: I stopped going out on the weekends, stopped doing anything other than what I had to do for school or softball. I continued to dig deeper into a hole of isolation—I felt guilty being around anyone else because all I could think about was how sad or frustrated I was. I broke up with my boyfriend at the time and stopped calling my family on a regular basis. I was actively ignoring the tiny voice inside that wanted help. I let her drown.

I was 100 percent in a downward spiral. This became a mental health issue over time, rather than just a mental game problem of being able to "flush it" or to focus. I felt very alone, and it's only after looking back that I truly see what I did to myself.

I knew why I did this. I felt like I wasn't contributing to the team as I wanted to, so I shut myself off from discussing the game or my feelings with teammates, not wanting to bring them down or be a burden. The same applied to my family; I would ignore calls from my mom and dad when they checked in on me. The last thing I wanted was someone asking, "How are you doing?" because it would send me into a breakdown.

I felt this way for months.

Always on the edge of losing it, crying because I was wound so tight.

Anything could trigger a cascade of more negativity. I was my own worst enemy.

Every problem felt so big. Every issue felt so heavy.

Normally, the holidays at home would help me gain some perspective, but not this year. I chose not to open up to them at home and instead kept holding my breath. From the moment I got back to Seattle from Christmas break at home, it felt like I had my foot on the gas, pushing to go forward, but I could only go further down.

The regular season starts in February, and you normally don't stop until May for the postseason. We had won the national championship just the year before, so everyone was watching us. And it truly felt like everyone saw me fail again and again.

HOW CAN YOU AVOID THIS?

If I could give one piece of advice to anyone struggling, it would be this: don't fight your battles alone. Reach out to your family, friends, or anyone who can help you disconnect from the negative thoughts and self-talk that lead to isolation. Even though it might feel like a big push to open up—especially because you fear being a burden to others—the people you trust often want nothing more than to connect with you and help you through your struggles.

From experience, the only thing that helped me *get out* of this time was reconnecting with my family.

Eventually, with time in a different space and the ability to let go, the issues that once felt so monumental began to shrink. I realized that my isolation had exaggerated what started as simple struggles with performing. Compared to everything else in my life, not hitting was not as catastrophic as I had made it out to be. The real issue was feeling alone. Not having anyone to talk to or any outlet for my feelings or thoughts became overwhelming.

LESSON TWO: WHEN YOU DON'T FEEL SAFE, EVERYTHING WILL FEEL LIKE AN ATTACK

During my junior year, I lived with four roommates in a house we called "the Brick." You can probably guess that it was a cute brick house, crowded inside with all of us. The house was on one of the main streets leading to campus and was pretty busy all the time. When football had a home game, we would have to park our cars up on the lawn so we wouldn't get a ticket for parking on the street.

During the school week, we had a routine for sharing parking passes and coordinating rides to the field. This was a far cry from the perks today's college athletes receive, such as paid parking passes and extra food. Our daily routine was so predictable that it made our movements easily trackable for someone watching our house.

On a regular afternoon, a group text came through from Marnie (one of my roommates): *"Looks like someone broke in. I called the cops. They are on their way."*

Within sixty seconds of that text, I was getting a call from another roommate, Taylor, who knew I was out of class. We both wanted to go home and check on the house. *How could this have happened? Why did it happen? What did this mean?*

Taylor and I parked and climbed the few stairs to the front door. I had my key in my hand as a habit to scoot past her to unlock it, but when I looked up, she was staring back at me with no words.

We had both seen the police car parked in the driveway, but now, as we stood at the wide-open door, our living room was unrecognizable. Couches moved around, the TV was missing, and the window was wide open. It had been sprinkling outside, so inside was now getting humid, and the smell of sweat was everywhere.

It didn't feel like our place. People had been in here, uninvited, with bad intentions.

As we moved through the house, other roommates arrived and took in the house too. Each of us gave details to the officers on site. Each of us went into our own rooms to inspect what was missing, what was damaged, what was different.

Downstairs, where my room was, the smell was worse. A window had been broken in my room. This must have been where they came in. It was musty, and the second I walked in, I knew I'd need to wash everything in there. I didn't know if I'd be able to sleep there.

The one place where I could escape trying to "fake it" and just let myself be... had been where they'd broken in. It was a daunting thought: these people had watched us, had known when we wouldn't be home, and had acted on it.

Our championship rings had been stolen.

TVs, jewelry... gone. The beds were overturned, random lamps knocked over, and jars broken on the path out the door.

After talking to the police, I stood outside, feeling as though this was the last thing anyone had expected. All I wanted was to go back to when I could feel at least a little safe in my room, and now I didn't even have that.

I called my mom to tell her, and her response was another thing I couldn't handle: over-the-top emotional and worried. Of course, she wanted to know every detail.

Having our rings stolen felt metaphoric to me in what I was going through: just last year was one of the happiest times of my life, and now... it felt as if that never happened. I was already not safe from my own self-talk; now my actual safety was in question, and it felt like another attack I was just trying to survive.

When you think things can't get any worse, they do—until you finally change something. This situation only reinforced my feeling that I needed to protect myself repeatedly—not just from the break-in, but also from everything I thought we had worked for, including that championship ring. Winning had given me confidence, and losing it left me feeling exposed.

The house was a mess, with broken windows, and I felt like my privacy had been violated. This mirrored how I felt inside—like everything I had built and hidden, including my lack of confidence, was now out in the open. My success in the 2009 World Series seemed irrelevant against this backdrop, and I felt compelled to repair everything.

STILL UNDER ATTACK

After the break-in, I tried to take some steps to recover.

My coaches encouraged me to see a mental performance coach and also to seek personal therapy. Mid-season, this was my attempt to rebuild myself and overcome the feeling of being broken and alone.

Our team worked with Ken Ravizza, a well-known mental performance coach, professor at Cal State Fullerton, author of *Heads-Up Baseball*, and consultant to professional baseball players.

After observing us as a team, my coaches selected a few players, including me, for individual phone calls with him. I know what this meant: they were worried about me.

I remember seeing Ken's number pop up on my phone. Coach Tarr had given me a heads-up that he would be calling, so I was expecting it. But thoughts still raced through my head: *I must really be bad if Coach Tarr thinks I need help from this guy. What do I say? Should I be honest about how I feel? No, he's a mental game guy; he just wants to figure out how to help me hit better, that's all anyone cares about, anyway. Don't waste the coaches' money.*

The call came as I was walking into dinner at Conibear Shellhouse. The Shellhouse provided weekly dinners for scholarship athletes from all sports. People were constantly walking in and out. It wasn't packed with kids yet, but when I pressed the button to answer the call, I was very aware that it was a place my teammates might be walking through or where other athletes I knew from soccer or volleyball might be. I knew I'd try to talk quietly.

When I answered, Ken was upbeat, and he led the conversation. I'm sure he was used to talking to athletes who weren't quite sure how to approach this type of talk.

He mentioned that Coach Tarr had told him I was someone the team really needed that year.

Worries overwhelmed me again. *What is he expecting me to tell him —to commit to?* Normally, when I became overwhelmed, I defaulted to trying to make the other person feel less uncomfortable than I was feeling, so my response was something like, "Yes! I want to work on being better for my team."

We went back and forth, talking about some of the content he'd brought up in the team session. He asked about my understanding of that and then pushed into my specific issues about hitting, saying, "So, what's up this year? How can I help best? You were a rockstar at the World Series, and it seems like something is holding you up. Want to talk about that a little bit?"

Again, the questions started: *What does he really know? I bet Coach Tarr told him I'm doing so badly that she doesn't know what to do with me. I can't believe I'm in this situation. What do I even say?*

I ended up simply saying that I just wasn't hitting well. I didn't open up. I didn't figure anything out that day. It was just another example of me protecting others from some of the more true thoughts I was having. I worked to keep them out.

Looking back, I know that if I had been in a different mindset, I might have seen this call as a compliment that Coach Tarr considered me important enough to recommend for help. However, at that point, it was hard for me to accept any assistance because I was already feeling so low.

How I was on that call was one of the many signs I missed. Thinking about how I couldn't sulk alone after the break-in. My inability to sleep. The constant replay of failures in my head. Coach Tarr's concern. Early warning signs were there, and I ignored all of them.

LESSON THREE: IGNORING THE SIGNS IS A WASTE OF TIME

Since we were the number-one-ranked team in the country, the team performed well despite my struggles throughout the year. For the second year in a row, we did what every college team hopes to do at the end of the season: we made it to the World Series.

By the time we were on the bus, taking that same exit to Hall of Fame Stadium (as it was called back in 2010), my brain was already seeing the little moments—the fond memories of the year before—differently, or I wasn't seeing them at all.

I had a lot of examples in my head of me failing from the regular season that year. I played scenes in my head of at-bats where I felt I didn't belong, and I thought about the teammates that should have been getting chances but weren't because I was playing instead. I remember one at-bat where I was taking a sign from my coach, and a fan in the stands stood up to try to get the crowd going. He said, "Let's do the cheer from back when she was good!"

That hurt and stuck with me.

It felt like all the bad things just kept sticking, and I didn't have any more room for good or even neutral. I couldn't be in the moment with my teammates because I was so angry at myself for not being able to shift into a different gear.

Not surprisingly, I can hardly remember anything from the 2010 World Series compared to the 2009 Series.

In 2009, one of my favorite routines (one that has always been a sort of tradition for teams competing in the Women's College World Series) was walking from the outfield gate, along the tall padded wall, toward the dugout. On this walk, teams get a first look at the field they saw on TV as kids. The smell of the dirt was like crayons. Your adrenaline would start pumping as you entered the spot where all the crowd noise had been coming from.

As you walked, younger fans reached down to high-five you, and some got quick autographs. My favorite thing to do as a player was to look up at the assigned section for our fans and find my family. First, I'd find my mom, then my dad, and I'd quickly smile and wave at others I recognized.

The World Series is bracket-style play, where the number of games you play depends on whether you win or lose. We won our first game, sending us into the winner's bracket. We won our second game, sending us to the semi-finals.

The semis were a battle, but we made it through, and I was flying high, leading the team in average, doubles, and hits.

I have three incredibly vivid memories from 2009:

1. My game-winning hit against ASU that sent us to the semi-finals, and seeing my hitting coach, who celebrated with me because he was there in person to see the whole thing.
2. The moment before the last pitch of the World Series, when I looked around the infield at my teammates and knew—*we had done it!*
3. Walking up that padded wall toward the dugout right before the Championship Series, thinking I was about to see the same faces, and I made eye contact with Johnny, my youngest brother. He had flown from California to Oklahoma City with our family friends (the Hamms) to surprise me and support our team. When I saw him, I

choked on the peanut butter pretzel I always ate on the walk and started crying. Happy tears. Coach Tarr noticed and right away asked me what was wrong. I was fine. I rushed into the dugout to get a grip, but seeing my brother while living out my dream of competing and winning a national championship filled me with so much joy I could have exploded.

2010'S STARK CONTRAST

I only have one concrete memory from the 2010 Women's College World Series.

I can't recall playing in any specific game, walking onto the field, or even striking out. The brain can be really strange and, at times, frightening. The only vivid memory I have from the second time my team made it to the WCWS is crying into my dad's chest outside the stadium once it was all over.

I had never done that before. Throughout that season, I had been ignoring my parents' calls, trying to shield them from seeing how poorly I was doing. But standing outside that stadium, I couldn't hold it in anymore.

I thought I was protecting them, but in reality, I must have been worrying them even more.

I cried with relief that the season was over, from the regret I felt at wasting an entire year, from exhaustion at beating myself up for months.

People were staring. I was sobbing—loudly, not being able to hide it.

When I got a chance to breathe, I thought, *I shouldn't even be crying. When I had the chance to do something in the game, I couldn't.*

And when I looked around, I "knew" my teammates and their parents were thinking the same thing. People were angry. We had just arrived in Oklahoma City, played two games, and were going home. The team ranked number one in the country for the majority of the year, the team with the MVP from last year was out.

I was convinced that these people (my teammates, coaches, all the families) were looking at me in disgust. They weren't wondering why I was crying; they were angry that I was. Maybe they were thinking the same thing I was about myself. Or maybe they honestly didn't care that I was upset—they thought that I deserved it. These were all things my inner voice was telling me.

A few moments after I started crying, relief morphed into guilt. I questioned why I deserved to feel better when I hadn't even contributed positively to the team. There were so many people on the bench who would have given anything to have been in my position.

So, I felt relief, I felt guilt, and then, finally, came the regret of having wasted an opportunity.

I hear that happens all the time.

WHAT DID I MISS?

I think I overlooked small parts of my daily life. If there's one overarching thing I ignored, it was my self-talk. I didn't realize how much it mattered. The narrative I was telling myself about expectations, about people judging me—from the way I was hard on myself at practice all the way to how I imagined my teammates' parents were thinking of me after the World Series—I was making the situation much worse with that story. My poor self-talk perpetuated a negative experience throughout the year.

In reality, I was fortunate that the season had a way to reset. After the postseason, I got to go home, set new goals, and truly understand what had happened. I continued to go to therapy and came to grips with how I had blocked out those difficult memories, as that time had been traumatic for me—not just because I wasn't hitting but because I felt completely unprotected, as if I were all on my own.

That year was particularly tough for me off the field, too—I lost two grandparents and faced relationship issues. A lot can happen while you're figuring out who you are, and it can be dangerous without a baseline of self-confidence or even neutral self-talk to navigate through it.

I think I got so deep into negativity that what started as a mental game issue—one that 99.9 percent of athletes experience at some point—became a mental health issue because I let everything spiral out of control. My performance affected my mood, my next play, and the pressure I felt. I eventually realized I needed to shift my focus back to what truly mattered.

RECOGNIZE THE WARNING SIGNS:

1. Negative self-talk. If your internal dialogue is negative, if you feel like a victim, or if you believe that things will never improve, that's something you need to address—and it can be fixed. It doesn't have to be fake self-talk.

2. Isolation. Negative self-talk can lead to isolation because you may not want to be vulnerable or let others in, feeling as though you need to protect them from your struggles.
3. Being unable to let go of your performance on the field. If you don't have an identity outside of how you perform, or if you care so much about what others think that it prevents you from engaging in conversations or activities unrelated to the game, that's definitely concerning.

WHAT CAN BE DONE IF YOU FEEL THAT SPORTS ARE AFFECTING YOUR MENTAL HEALTH?

Move Your Body

One thing I love to do now, which I wish I'd done more of back then, is to be more active with my body, because it truly affects my mind.

I started noticing that right after I got home, or in the morning, even before my day began, I would spend a lot of time sitting still, alone with my thoughts in my room.

As I grew older, I learned that engaging in more physical activity —such as yoga, hiking, walking, or doing a short strength workout —helped my mind and body. Moving around and getting away from negative thoughts about myself was essential. It's important to break out of your routine, rather than relying solely on team workouts.

There is a lot of science behind how physical activity can boost serotonin and dopamine levels—chemicals in the brain that enhance our mood. When we feel better, we tend to make better choices regarding our self-talk and our interactions with others. This positive state can significantly influence our mental health.

Connect with Family or Friends

I also recommend scheduling time to connect with family members. Reflecting on my junior year, I regret not having more moments with my mom. I lost that time, and I could have used her support to help me manage my feelings. She had the ability to see me, which would have alleviated my sense of isolation. It doesn't have to be a parent; anyone who makes you feel connected can make a difference. Making a genuine effort to reach out and engage with others is crucial for breaking free from negative thoughts.

Try Therapy

Even if you're not experiencing a mental health crisis, it can be incredibly beneficial to seek advice from a mental health professional. Talking through your thoughts and experiences with someone who provides a safe space can be immensely helpful. Therapists are bound to confidentiality and won't share what you discuss with them. In my experience, therapy provides a reflective space where you can articulate your feelings and hear them echoed back to you. This process allows you to pause and reconsider how you define your thoughts and stories.

Therapy is an excellent way to interrupt negative thought patterns before they escalate. Many schools provide access to mental performance coaches or therapists for student-athletes, which is a great resource worth exploring.

Write It Down

When I put my thoughts on paper, I can see how far I've come, which is empowering. Starting to journal during my junior year and continuing after graduation has been eye-opening. On tough days, documenting my feelings serves as a reminder that I can eventually find meaning in my experiences. While many people may dislike the phrase "everything happens for a reason," I find it comforting during dark times, particularly when I am struggling with feelings of worthlessness.

Please Read If You've Felt Worthless:

There are times when certain topics are avoided in books for young athletes because we don't want to expose them to those ideas. However, the reality is that there are some repetitive, hurtful thoughts and traumatic experiences that can lead to severe mental health issues, including thoughts of suicide. This isn't normal, and when it happened to me, I felt so alone because I truly believed I *was* alone. It is incredibly scary to be the only one who knows your thoughts, especially when your thoughts betray you. Especially when you know that if you told anyone, they would be scared too.

If this ever happens to you, please seek help. No matter how embarrassed, proud, or unsure you may feel about whether people can help you, reach out. You are not your thoughts, and when those thoughts begin to mislead you into darkness, it is critical to recognize it and ask for support.

Those feelings and experiences during dark times can be incredibly painful, but that pain can also lead to valuable lessons later in life—*but* only if you don't let them sink you by staying alone. If we have the patience to see that, we can find meaning in our struggles, and our lives can improve significantly.

Journaling, in particular, allows us to process our thoughts. There's a powerful connection between thoughts and words; when we put our thoughts into writing, they can evolve into actions. Writing can serve as a pause for reflection, enabling us to reread what we're experiencing. Many people struggle to share their feelings in therapy or to be vulnerable. It can be easier to share what we've written or read it back, rather than just saying we are fine when that's not the truth. Journaling can give us the courage to express ourselves.

There's a lot of positive that has emerged from my experiences as a college athlete and my willingness to share those darker moments. In those moments, it really didn't feel like the darkness would end, but I promise you it does. My hope is that you keep moving through the worst times if you're there (or end up there in the future). There's more for you coming, and a whole lot of people who are depending on you to make it there.

MY PERSONAL STAT SHEET

1. Processing emotions alone magnifies everything.

> 1/10. This year, I did everything alone. I was mean to myself, scared... I had always been taught to be independent and that I could figure anything out. But in this case, if I had opened up and been a little bit vulnerable, it might have made my problems easier to manage.

2. When you don't feel safe, everything will feel like an attack.

3/10. A huge theme for me in my junior year was safety. I wasn't even safe in my own head, so I was often in fight-or-flight mode, if not the entire time.

3. Ignoring the signs is a waste of time.

1/10. From the moment I started feeling pressure and the weight of expectation, I could have been working on my self-talk and focusing on the process instead of only the results. There were so many signs to ask for help, and I should have taken them seriously. I knew they were serious, but taking action on them was the step I lacked. I didn't know where to turn

CHAPTER 5
SENIOR YEAR

MY PLAYER STAT SHEET *2011 (Senior)*
• Named to the Capital One Academic All-American District VIII team
• Earned Honorable Mention All-Pac-10 honors
• Appeared and started in all 53 games at third base
• Batted .271, collecting 39 hits in 144 at-bats with 39 runs, three doubles, two triples, seven home runs, 29 RBIs, and a .414 on-base percentage
• Fielding percentage was .940 with 116 assists (tied for most on team).

RUMINATING ABOUT THE FUTURE WHILE HIDING IN THE PRESENT

I thought I had learned my lesson.

After hitting what I believed was my lowest point junior year, I went home that summer to reset. I trained, spent time with family, and promised myself I'd never sink that low again. When I returned for my senior year, I made changes. I moved out of my old place and into the softball house—a choice I'd turned down as a sophomore when Coach Tarr suggested the "disciplined" option, the Brick, would send a better message. This time, I chose differently.

I was done running from potential outcomes. I wanted to discover who I could be regardless of my performance in sports—to pursue what made me happy rather than fear what might happen.

I thought the problem had been about softball: pressure, expectations, my inability to handle failure. So I fixed those external things. I trained harder. I changed my environment. I changed my mindset.

But I had missed something crucial. The real lesson wasn't about softball at all. It was about self-acceptance, about feeling safe with myself, about not seeking external validation to define who I should be. But I didn't get it yet, and that showed up in my senior season.

LESSON ONE: THE LESSONS WE DON'T LEARN KEEP RESURFACING

It was Halloween. Even though I didn't really "go out" anymore because I had learned that alcohol and my goals didn't mix, I made an exception because I had also made a resolution not to overthink everything. My team was going out, and I wanted to go, too.

Anything that put me around people and in a good headspace was where I wanted to be.

We all met at an apartment, and the vibes quickly shifted from a team hangout to different groups wanting to break off. I found myself with just a couple of others mixing up whipped cream vodka and orange juice and finding *Hocus Pocus* on TV. I remember falling asleep in a teammate's bed and then hearing knocks on the door and laughter.

In the morning, I woke up and felt my hand holding another hand. I slowly opened my eyes to see my teammate asleep beside me. My thoughts started racing immediately. *What had happened? Who else had seen this? This was so wrong. I let my guard down for one second, and this?*

I got up and snuck out to find the bathroom. I was wearing a shirt that wasn't mine. I looked in the bathroom mirror; my eyes were puffy, with makeup still on them. *What had I done?*

In that moment of panic and shame, I should have recognized what was happening. The familiar feeling of *this is so wrong,* washing over me. The immediate impulse to hide, to keep secrets, to handle everything alone in my head.

These were the exact warning signs I had learned to recognize junior year. But I didn't see them as the same yet.

When I went back to get my keys and wallet, my teammate was sitting up. "You feeling okay?" she asked, laughing. If she was feeling awkward or mortified, like me, she was doing a really good job of hiding it.

I stumbled on my words: "My head hurts a little. I need some food, ha-ha."

She walked me out and hugged me. "So, last night got a little crazy... Maybe we can talk about it when we are feeling better."

She approached it so lightly, as though she were fine with not knowing how this would turn out. Or was she waiting for me to give my opinion first? She also seemed to really like me, and even though my initial feelings ranged from horrified to embarrassed to angry with myself, they faded into the background because she seemed to be okay with it, and maybe I liked her too.

A part of me thought that I had never allowed myself to do anything that wasn't "perfect" or right, and maybe I could actually relax and just have fun. Maybe this would help me?

Our talk turned into more hanging out, which turned into a "situationship" with a teammate. My actual feelings for her got more serious. There was a lot of sneaking and lying about what was going on. Neither of us wanted this to be public, so we weren't exclusive. This led to jealousy, sadness, and unjustified anger when I saw her at parties with guys, or even dating some of them. Before I knew it, this light and fun fling turned toxic.

What started as an exciting secret for the fall turned into another way I would isolate myself, unable to manage my own self-talk, and this became a new source of what made me really not like myself. I was living a secret and accepting pretty terrible treatment.

And just like that, I was back in the pattern.

Different circumstances: instead of hiding how hard I was on myself, I was now hiding other parts of myself. I was processing everything alone again, and just like junior year taught me, processing alone magnifies everything.

This secret, filled with doubt about whether it was right or wrong, led to hesitations in my personal life that affected everything else. I felt confused, unworthy, and sad a lot of the time in private, all while putting on a front as a strong, stable senior leader without any worries.

Junior year, I isolated because I felt like a burden; like my struggles with performance would drag my teammates down. Senior year, I isolated because I felt like a secret—like what I was doing would make people judge me. The context changed, but the pattern didn't.

This would impact my play, my overall mindset (always thinking about being found out), and my relationship with my family because I wasn't only hiding this from my team and everyone at school. Now I was hiding from everyone at home for a much deeper reason.

When I thought I was at my lowest in my junior year (the thing I was so adamant about avoiding), I managed to escape self-doubt once I went home. I was able to reset, based on the promise that I would improve my performance and no longer have to hide in my head.

Now...

I found myself hiding my feelings again and grappling with self-hatred. Despite deciding over the summer that I would never allow myself to feel that low again, I was deep in a struggle internally. It was worse now because I was questioning everything about myself, feeling like the questions would never end.

I "knew" I couldn't tell anyone. I knew I was really starting to struggle. I started getting really bad thoughts about harming myself or just disappearing so that I didn't have to be so miserable anymore.

This should have terrified me. This was the same dark place I'd been junior year—the place I swore I'd never return to. But instead of recognizing the pattern, I looked for a different external solution.

Out of desperation, I went to church in search of refuge and guidance.

Looking back, I can see what I was really doing. I wasn't genuinely seeking spiritual education. I was looking for someone else to give me the answer—to tell me what was right or wrong, so I didn't have to do the hard internal work of figuring out who I was and what I believed.

Junior year, I sought validation through performance. Senior year, I sought validation through the Church. Same pattern, different disguise.

I had never been overtly taught that what I was doing was wrong, but I knew the Catholic Church didn't believe in it. I wanted to learn about why this was, but mostly... I wanted a black-and-white answer. I wanted the Church to give me a good enough reason to end a relationship I already knew was toxic. I was seeking external validation instead of trusting my own internal compass—instead of accepting that I needed to give myself time and grace to figure things out.

I started Confirmation classes with the hope that I would find the determination to stop a relationship I knew was hurting me.

Looking back, I see where I was mentally: I was scared and thought what I was doing was wrong. I didn't want to be judged by others and, maybe most of all, didn't want to be caught caring more about a person who ultimately thought what we were doing was wrong, too. Instead of doing the work to figure out what it meant for me, I just wanted a "known." I masked that as trying to learn more and educate myself about right and wrong.

I went through the entire Confirmation process, and many teammates came to support me during the ceremony. I remember feeling a sense of accomplishment because I had attended these classes consistently. However, I also felt like I was living a lie; I felt wrong. The main lesson I took away was not that I found the answer I needed, but rather that the path I chose for education created more anxiety and a sense that I could never fully accept myself.

I want to be clear: this wasn't the Church's fault. Faith communities provide incredible support, guidance, and belonging for so many people—including many of my friends and students who have found real peace and purpose through their faith. The problem wasn't the Church or its teachings. The problem was my mindset walking in. I wasn't genuinely seeking spiritual growth or community—I was trying to outsource a decision I needed to make for myself. I wanted the Church to tell me what to do so I wouldn't have to do the hard internal work of figuring out who I was and what I believed.

When you approach anything—faith, therapy, coaching, advice from friends—from a place of "please just tell me what to do," you're not really seeking guidance. You're seeking an escape from taking responsibility for your own life.

The *biggest* lesson I kept missing: Until you accept yourself, until you feel safe with who you are, the same patterns will keep showing up—just in different forms.

My acceptance of myself has been crucial. I've learned to take things day by day and to experience life, rather than constantly judging myself and accepting judgment from others. It took me a long time, even beyond college, to actually give myself grace. I had to see the pattern repeat—junior year isolation about softball, senior year isolation about identity—before I understood: the lesson wasn't about the specific situation. It was about learning to feel safe with myself, to process with others, and to trust my own internal guidance instead of constantly seeking external validation.

How Did I Eventually Move Forward From This?

To be honest, my internal strength and discipline just weren't strong enough to make good choices for me. I had to physically take myself out of situations that hurt me. As you'll read about later on, I moved home not only for job reasons, but also for mental health reasons.

A Note About This Pattern

My story is about questioning my identity and hiding a relationship, but this pattern shows up everywhere. Maybe you're hiding academic struggles, mental health issues, family problems, substance use, or relationship troubles. The specifics don't matter

—what matters is recognizing when you're isolating yourself, seeking external validation to make decisions for you, and living in fear of judgment. That's the pattern.

What I Wish I'd Done Differently

If I could go back, I would:

- Tell at least *one* trusted person what I was going through (didn't have to be everyone)— this shouldn't have impacted me so deeply... looking back, it wasn't *that* big of a deal.
- Tell a therapist the truth: I would fib the couple of times I sought out a therapist, not wanting to be completely honest about how bad it was.
- Remember that giving yourself time to figure things out isn't the same as hiding. You can say "I'm still figuring this out" without secrecy and shame.

LESSON TWO: WORRYING DOES NOTHING

Throughout my senior year, I viewed everything as a series of lasts. This was my last fall ball, my last warm-up, my last time at this stadium. I became so preoccupied with the uncertainty of my future and who I would be after softball that I started to focus on all the things that worried me.

You would think that recognizing these as "lasts" would make me think, *I have nothing to lose. I want to soak everything in.* Right after that moment of awareness, it turned into worry. I felt anxious about what was coming next because I'd always had a softball season to look forward to. That familiarity was a great comfort to me.

When I thought about what life would be like after graduating from college, that feeling of uncertainty was amplified a hundredfold. Suddenly, I would have to support myself and learn how things like insurance, taxes, and real jobs worked. The worry and doubt overshadowed the significance of my final games and team dinners. My need to navigate the challenges of adult life felt so pressing. I didn't want to move back home with my parents or ask for help; I had always been someone who thrived on knowing what would happen next. But this was territory I had no experience in at all.

With two months left in my senior year, I was deeply absorbed in that toxic relationship. I often used it as a distraction from the fear of the unknown that lay ahead. A lot of the events I experienced during my senior year—whether it was drama on the team or other challenges I faced—felt like they were distractions from this unsettling uncertainty.

As I approached my senior day, I felt preoccupied with so many things, and I didn't feel fully included in my family's plans to travel from California to Washington to be part of my senior weekend. I was so busy going through future scenarios, the weekend snuck up on me. In total, about fifteen family members were present on that day... it felt like one minute I was living my regular college life and the next minute they were all there, bringing the version of me that I was when I was with them, too.

My mom had somehow organized aunts, cousins, and godparents to come and see me, even without my help with the details.

My aunts and their families, all my younger cousins, were in Washington T-shirts, either an oversized one I had given them or one they had gotten from the bookstore.

We all lined up outside the downstairs gate that led us out to the third-base side of the field. I looked around and saw Jenn and her family, and Ashley and her family (the other seniors who would be walking out as part of the senior day ceremony). My mom and dad were on either side of me, holding my hands as we walked out in front of the crowd during my introduction.

Over the speakers, I heard my stats being announced. They started with freshman year, spent a long time on what I had done my sophomore year as a part of the National Championship team, and then I stopped listening, as I knew there wouldn't be anything good for the rest.

There's a photo of my mom waving up to the stands as we start walking out, while my gaze is fixed forward. I'm smiling, and my dad is on my other side, and we stay holding hands as we walk toward the pitcher's mound for the whole crowd to give us a hand.

I only looked up briefly; mainly, I just looked forward to the line of my teammates ready to give hugs and shed a couple of tears for our last regular-season home game.

My emotions definitely didn't match the visuals of that day. On the outside, I wanted to appear put-together to everyone, but internally, I was struggling.

I remember feeling enveloped in a haze of distraction, worry, and fear. Despite knowing I should be so happy and that it should be a celebratory occasion, I often felt numb. In pictures from that day, I do appear happy—smiling and surrounded by people who were genuinely proud of me. However, I wasn't fully present. I was hiding a secret relationship and, despite all this pride around me, I knew I hadn't played to my potential. I wasn't happy and felt like these proud people didn't quite know me.

I found myself caught up in a cycle of thoughts, trying to prepare for the worst-case scenarios: *What if I don't have a job after this? What if I have to take care of myself? What if I have to ask for help?*

I think I worried as a way to protect myself from disappointment or from others' judgment. On senior day, surrounded by my peers and their families, I was overwhelmed by regret for having wasted time worrying.

I've realized that thinking about the worst-case scenario only makes you right once—it doesn't lead to happiness. Throughout the year, I was so busy worrying that I missed out on simply living in the moment.

What I should have done instead: When worry started spiraling, pause and ask: *Is this worry helping me prepare, or is it just stealing my joy?* Most of the time, it was stealing. Instead of catastrophizing about the future, I should have focused on what I could control in that moment—showing up, being present, and actually experiencing the "lasts" instead of just dreading them.

LESSON THREE: YOU MATTER—KNOW YOUR VALUE

My final game as a college athlete took place at the University of Missouri—on their home turf, where we weren't supposed to win. We were underdogs. The year before, we'd been ranked number one at the World Series and got knocked out in two games. Now our star pitcher was gone, and as a senior, I tried to stand tall for my freshman pitcher and the rest of the team.

But something was off.

As a third baseman, I've always been confident on defense. Throwing is one of the most controllable parts of the game—you've already adjusted to the unknowns, controlled the chaos. Once the ball is in your glove, the throw is something you can control.

Except I couldn't.

During this series, I had the "yips"—where a player completely loses control of their throws. It's mental, not physical. Your body knows how to throw, but your brain won't let you.

During warm-ups, I nearly hit an umpire twice. I'd grip the ball, feel my feet hit the ground *right, left,* but the ball would sail either way left or way right.

It felt metaphoric: I'd spent all year hiding, and now, even when I was trying to lead from my safe place on defense, the one thing I could always control—was gone. I was trying my best to lead with what I had, but the train had gone off the tracks.

The Final Out

Going into the last inning, we were losing. Top of the seventh. I knew if we didn't tie or take the lead, it was over.

I went to the plate thinking, *Don't strike out.*

I had an "okay" at-bat—hit the ball up the middle, got on base. Victoria Hayward came up with two outs. She hit it to the second baseman. I tried to backpedal to avoid the tag, but I knew she was too close. She ran me down and tagged me hard in the gut.

That was it. The final out. My time as a student-athlete was done.

I looked to the dugout and jogged back. Missouri was celebrating. I focused on my teammates, glanced up at my mom in the stands —the only family who'd come. Some teammates were crying.

I felt nothing.

It was as if all my thoughts and preparations for how I *should* feel in that moment prevented me from actually experiencing it. The logical part took over: *Okay, you're done. Pack up. Make your teammates feel better.*

The Realization

When I got back to the dugout, she was still crying.

Not about the loss. Not about my final game. She'd been crying throughout the game because she wasn't playing. The teammate I'd been in this secret, toxic relationship with—during *my* final game ever—was crying about herself.

Instead of noticing the weight of my moment, instead of being supportive... I finally saw her clearly.

She was obsessed with her playing time, her image, how coaches and teammates perceived her. Her behavior wasn't about me—it was about her and her own struggles.

And seeing her clearly helped me start seeing myself clearly, if only for a moment.

I'd been consumed by what she thought of me, how I'd show up for her, whether I was doing enough. I'd let her self-absorption convince me I didn't matter. Beyond her, I was consumed with what so many other people thought of me, too. But standing there in that dugout, watching her cry about herself during my final game, something clicked:

I deserved to be treated better. To be considered. Not just by her... but by myself too. Not because it was "my turn" to be upset, but because I mattered too.

The realization came too late to change how I experienced that game. But it was the first step toward understanding my own value.

The Interview

After the game, I was called into the post-game interview with reporters, alongside another senior teammate and Coach Tarr. Coach was visibly upset. Jenn held back tears. Their answers were short but heartfelt.

When I answered questions, I spoke in a joking tone. I laughed about a ball that was called foul during the game, looked around hoping others would laugh with me. It didn't match the gravity of the situation—we'd just been eliminated.

I look back at that interview and don't recognize myself.

This version of me didn't recognize my own value. I was shielding myself and others from the heaviness I knew was creeping in. I wanted to move through this important moment so quickly instead of feeling it all.

I was just done. I'd spent too much time consumed by expectations—trying not to worry my parents, putting too much power into a relationship, seeking approval from coaches, performing at the cost of my mental health. I wish I'd gotten to experience my last game as *me*: the kid who'd worked so hard to get there and deserved to be proud of that work.

What I Learned Too Late

That realization, looking in the dugout—that I deserved better treatment from myself—should have come much sooner.

Throughout my college career, I was exhausting myself trying to look okay on the outside. People who loved me knew I wasn't fine, but I wasn't open to talking. I wanted to present myself as a strong leader—someone without issues, reliable, independent. My version of a leader didn't have secrets, self-hate, or doubt.

But inside, that wasn't me at all.

I devalued myself for months—years, really. I placed others' judgments above my own needs. I accepted terrible treatment because I didn't believe I deserved better. I performed the role of "strong senior leader" while barely holding myself together.

My regret isn't about my choice of school or even my performance on the field. It's that I settled for looking fine instead of actually being well. I gave so much energy to managing everyone else's perception of me that I lost sight of my own experience.

WHAT KNOWING YOUR VALUE ACTUALLY LOOKS LIKE

Don't wait until the final out to realize you spent your entire career trying to look fine instead of actually being well.

Knowing your value means:

- **Not accepting treatment that diminishes you**—whether from a relationship, a coach, or your own inner voice
- **Asking for help instead of hiding**—even when you think leaders aren't supposed to struggle
- **Being present in your moments instead of performing for others**—your experience matters, not just how it looks

"Fine" is not the goal—thriving is. And thriving means treating yourself with the same consideration you'd give a teammate.

Give yourself grace, especially when it feels impossible. Grace doesn't mean lowering your standards. It means valuing yourself *more* than your need to look perfect—more than others' judgments, more than external validation, more than keeping secrets to protect your image.

MY PERSONAL STAT SHEET

1. The lessons we don't learn keep resurfacing.

> 2/10. I tried to make adjustments, but I didn't get the overall deeper message. It wasn't just about "being happy" and being around people. It was about being okay with the growth and being on your own team, no matter what.

2. Worrying does nothing; thinking "worst case" only makes you right once.

> 2/10. I wanted to control everything rather than be okay with the unknown, so I made up stories of all the worst ways things would turn out. This led me to overthink, not

reach out to others, and to make the worst-case scenarios come true.

3. You matter. Know your value.

1/10. I left college with a bad taste in my mouth. I felt burned out and ready to be done. Shrinking to make others comfortable affected me a lot. Constantly making myself smaller and not honoring what I needed exhausted me.

CHAPTER 6
POST-COLLEGE

MY PLAYER STAT SHEET

Post-College

- 2012 Riverside Sports Hall of Fame Inductee
- 2013 Professional Softball Player (Switzerland)
- 2013–2014 College Coach (UCR, LMU)
- 2014 Established my own lessons business
- 2014 University of Washington Hall of Fame Inductee
- 2015 & 2019 Filipino National Softball Team
- 2014–2020 Co-Founder of The Packaged Deal
- 2019–2025 Team Easton Ambassador
- 2024–present 200+ families attend my lessons weekly, hundreds of thousands reached over social media monthly, annual events where families, local and out of state, invest to bring their athletes to be positively impacted.

WHAT NOW?

Three months after my final out, I was sitting in a cubicle at 5 a.m... wondering how I'd gotten there.

After graduation, many athletes feel lost, believing they should have everything figured out. In reality, if you think you've got it all figured out, it might be because you don't have a goal or vision that's big enough.

This felt like a major reset, but I still didn't know what I wanted to do with my life. I had a sociology degree and was burned out from softball. I wanted a "big girl" job—something that would prove I was moving forward, that my college experience had been worth it.

I sought out something that would challenge me and connect me to my interests. I was trying to fill the void left by softball; I wanted to replicate the hard work I had put into that sport and find a sense of community.

LESSON ONE: SOMETIMES, STICKING IT OUT ISN'T THE BEST COURSE OF ACTION

After everything that happened senior year, the idea of studying sports psychology—my original plan—felt like a joke. How could I help athletes with their mental health when I'd hidden my own struggles for years? People asked if I'd coach. I wanted to run from softball, but it felt like the only thing I knew—that and the fact that I didn't want to move back in with my parents. Going backward felt like I was admitting defeat, like nothing I had gone through truly meant anything.

Jane, one of my friends from the soccer team, and I were graduating at the same time, and it felt like we were in the same boat. We had no idea what we should do now, but we both had degrees, weren't playing anymore, and didn't want to move home to California.

She had a friend whose mom worked in a significant role at the Fred Hutchinson Cancer Research Center on Lake Union, near downtown Seattle.

The hours were a little crazy because they were on East Coast time, 5 a.m. to 1 p.m., but we thought this could be a cool way to get job experience and start living a "real" Seattle life.

Jane applied for the interview and shared her connection with me, whom I reached out to. We both got emails back and helped each other pick out interview outfits. When the day came that we both had our interviews, we were both so nervous that we barely spoke.

Fortunately, a week later, we heard back. We'd both gotten the job.

This role involved working in a call center that opened at 8 a.m. Eastern Time, meaning we had to be ready for calls at 5 a.m. Pacific Time. Living in Seattle, this required us to wake up at 4 a.m., drive downtown in the dark, and be at our desks on time. The job also included about nine months of training because the call center's purpose was to assist patients, family members, and doctors with questions about cancer.

Coming out of college without any medical background or formal training, the idea of answering calls and playing the expert was intimidating. We were trained for months on how to find information, look up resources, and emotionally support callers, depending on where they were in their cancer journey. At times, we had to guide a child whose parent had just received a stage-four cancer diagnosis, helping them understand what that meant, which was really heavy emotionally.

During the training phase, the day-to-day was lighter but still challenging. We were engaged in learning, establishing a new routine, and developing an identity within this community. It felt more like school than a job. I definitely learned a lot about cancer during those months.

After the training period, we transitioned to answering calls, which created a completely different dynamic. The calls we received were intense, and because we started work so early in the day, by the time I got home, I was mentally and emotionally exhausted. I thought I would still have time and energy to work out, but instead, I often went to bed as soon as it got dark, which, in Seattle during the winter, could be as early as 6 or 7 p.m.

I realized that working at a desk was not for me. It was emotionally draining to have a job centered around such a heavy topic and be expected to give emotionally to complete strangers. During a time when I was still recovering from the traumatic experience of being a student-athlete, I simply didn't have the emotional capacity to handle it. I remember coming home for Christmas and sharing my experience with my family. I received two very different reactions from my parents.

One of the first significant conversations I had was with my dad. I've always seen him as a strong, steady, and constant figure in my life. He has worked in the same insurance job for many years, but I also related to him because he grew up playing football and, like me, received a scholarship to play his sport, which paid for his college.

From college, my dad was drafted by the Miami Dolphins. In training camp, he suffered a career-ending shoulder injury and had to find a job that would support him and my mom. In my mind, my dad knew what it was like to have your course altered by something unexpected, just like me.

So when I told him I was struggling at Fred Hutch, I thought he'd understand. Instead, he said... "Well, that's life. You may not enjoy your job, but you stick it out 'cause that's what you have to do."

He emphasized that having a steady income brings peace of mind and is something to be thankful for.

On the other hand, my mom's viewpoint was more typical of many mothers; she believed I could do no wrong. She saw my special gifts and encouraged me to find something that truly excited me. Her advice cut through: "Morgan, I know you. You're not afraid of working hard—you've never been afraid of that. Find something that energizes you, not something that drains you."

The hardest part for me was realizing that my job wasn't sustainable in terms of energy. I had never quit anything before, and as an athlete, admitting defeat and choosing to quit felt foreign. For weeks, I wrestled with the decision. As an athlete, quitting felt like admitting defeat. I'd never walked away from anything before. But when I finally gave my notice, something surprising happened: instead of guilt, I felt relief. A weight lifted. I could finally say "yes" to new opportunities that were better suited for me.

My mom was right. There's a difference between persevering through something hard that matters to you and grinding through something that's depleting you for the wrong reasons.

I'd spent four years as an athlete pushing through the wrong kind of hard—performing instead of healing, hiding instead of growing. I wasn't going to start my post-college life doing the same thing.

Leaving Fred Hutch wasn't quitting. It was the first time I chose myself.

LESSON TWO: CREATE YOUR OWN STATS

A year into my first college coaching job at Loyola Marymount, I was ten pounds heavier, dreading mornings, and spending maybe 15 percent of my time actually coaching. The rest was emails, recruiting calls, logistics, and traffic. I'd left one draining job for another.

The Problem

I should have been happy. I had a steady paycheck, I was coaching Division I softball, I was back in California near my family—except I barely saw them. I started dreading going to sleep because I knew I'd wake up to another day of the same thing. Sound familiar?

I was depleting myself again, doing something that didn't align with who I was or what I needed.

The difference this time? I'd learned something. I couldn't just push through anymore. I needed a different way to evaluate whether I should stay or go.

The Shift

In sports, we track everything: batting average, ERA, fielding percentage, RBIs. As a coach, it was recruiting class rankings and win-loss records. But none of those stats told me if I was actually *thriving*.

So I started tracking different things. Not performance metrics that others would judge me by, but measurements that reflected what actually mattered to me:

The Stats I Created

I started really paying attention to these things and trying to find measurements of each of them:

1. The time I spent actually doing the things I was passionate about.

> While most people see college coaching as just coaching, the majority of the actual work for me was recruiting, organizing trips, planning meetings, keeping athletes accountable to their classes, and answering emails. Not every experience is the same, depending on the size of your staff, but when I evaluated how much time I spent with athletes, in a flow, and getting them better... I came up with a number around 15 percent.

2. Time I had for family and growing myself outside of work.

> I loved the fact that this job was in California so that I could visit my family whenever I wanted. The key phrase turned

into "whenever I could" because, based on the hours of the job and the fact that traffic from LA started at noon, I would often be sitting in my car longer than I could hang out with them. Consequently, my trips to see family dwindled to never.

3. How much money I made.

This number only mattered to me because it was relevant to my living expenses: rent, food, and gas. I didn't think I'd need much, but this was a good baseline to aim for when I was looking for other options.

4. My overall health and hopefulness for the future.

Since starting the job, I had gained ten pounds and never had time to get into a regular workout routine. I always felt rushed and like I never quite finished what I had set out to do for myself the day before. This was the biggest red flag for me.

THE SIDE HUSTLE THAT TOLD THE TRUTH

While working at LMU, I started giving private lessons and traveling for clinics on weekends. Technically, another job. The travel was brutal. But those hours left me energized instead of depleted.

During LMU practices, I found myself thinking about new drills for my clinics, looking forward to weekends when I'd feel freer to create. The contrast was impossible to ignore.

By May, I'd done the math. Using lessons and clinics as my sole income might actually work. It was a risk. It was scary. But doing something that gave me energy—something I could grow—overshadowed the fear.

I left the job.

PROOF IT WORKED

That summer after I decided not to go back to LMU, I was invited to play for Team Philippines as they competed at the Asian Games. I hadn't played competitively since my last game in 2011 with Washington, so I was nervous about jumping back into that kind of intensity.

The timing was wild: when I was called to play, I only had a couple of days to decide. Our first tournament was in less than two weeks. I agreed to play and immediately started working out on the field again.

I was living a completely different life than I had been as a college coach just a couple of months before, and my body started to feel that way. I was moving more and eating better—not because I was tracking or stressing, but because I was doing things that energized me. I was eating to feel ready to play, practicing hard, competing.

The Asian Games were just a week long, in Incheon, South Korea. My plan was to play in those and then pour myself 100 percent into lessons when I was back. I wasn't focused on changing anything with my body. I was focused on playing and eating things that would help me feel ready to play.

When I came home from South Korea and showed up to teach lessons, a few people mentioned I looked like I'd lost weight. I stepped on the scale later: I'd lost all the weight I'd gained while coaching.

I felt lighter—not just physically, but like I'd shed the weight of doing things I wasn't meant to do.

That's when it clicked: I'd been measuring the wrong things my whole life. During college, I viewed stats as a way for others to judge me. After the Asian Games, I flipped the script. Stats became a tool for *me*—a way to understand my own growth and recreate what worked.

The shift isn't small. It's choosing to see your stats as tools instead of judgments. It's being secure enough in your effort to focus on your own progress, not everyone else's numbers.

This lesson is especially useful for athletes. Many of us grow up in competitive environments, constantly evaluating where we stand. When our time in competitive sports comes to an end, it's easy to fall out of routine with exercise and healthy eating.

HOW I USE THIS NOW

I have learned how much I enjoy creating my own metrics, especially around health and priorities. I do 30-day or 90-day challenges to jump-start habits and see change quickly, which then motivates longer stretches as well.

This doesn't mean I monitor myself every single day; sometimes, it's essential to take a break and simply be. But checking in has been helpful, especially considering how much weight I gained my freshman year in college. I always want to see how I'm doing every now and then instead of continuing if I'm unknowingly stuck in a bad habit.

Here's an example of a 30-Day Challenge I tried, implementing multiple themes:

- Last meal before 6 p.m.
- 20+ minute walk every morning
- No phone after lessons
- Strength workout three times per week
- 10,000 steps per day
- Call Mom one morning per week

Notice that last one? One of my top priorities is family. I've noticed that after conversations with my mom or time with my parents on weekends, I tend to have better weeks overall. So I started tracking: how often was I actually reaching out?

It's simple, but tracking connection with loved ones helps ensure I don't fall into isolating habits or let stress take over.

Imagine becoming so consumed by your goals or the stresses of life that you lose touch with your family, especially if you live away from them. If you later look back at your habits and realize, *I haven't reached out, haven't connected, haven't engaged with the people who matter to me,* you'll see that your stress and dissatisfaction may stem from not aligning your actions with your priorities.

YOUR STATS, YOUR LIFE

During your sports career, you may often reflect on your future and who you want to be. Much of that self-reflection revolves around your job, but I've heard from many students who have graduated that they often struggle with defining themselves and knowing how to navigate life after sports. This feeling is entirely normal.

There will come a time—though it varies for everyone, whether it's six months or five years—when you're trying to find your footing and gain experience outside of your sport.

You'll be exploring who you are without the constant scheduling, workouts, training, games, and practices that come with being an athlete. You'll need to get a job or figure out how to otherwise support yourself. In this process, you'll get more and more comfortable saying "yes" or "no" to different opportunities based on past experiences; you won't be so afraid of making the wrong choice each time.

Your stats don't need to mirror mine. A great exercise: list your priorities and values, then track habits that align with what matters most to you.

You'll have a void of time that used to be spent moving toward championships and personal records. Now you get to decide what you'll use your energy for. Give yourself time and space to explore. Be creative. What you're looking for might not be on the same path as others are taking.

Since starting my lesson business in 2014, I've built something that functions beyond just me. I filled the void of playing softball with teaching it—and this path isn't for everyone, but I hope you accept this challenge: find a job that gives you more energy than it takes.

MY PERSONAL STAT SHEET

1. Sticking it out sometimes isn't the best course of action

> 9/10. I feel that once I figured out that something wasn't for me, I moved on pretty quickly after college. I have also

been able to use my intuition to know when I should stay put.

2. You can make your own stats.

8/10. I am pretty good at this now, and I know I don't need to be perfect. Outside of competitive sports, the stats I keep for my wellness don't have to stay strict 100 percent of the time as long as I'm consistently plugging back in. Stats for my business or activities I want to be most competitive in... those stats should be more strictly kept.

FINAL THOUGHTS

If I could go back to that freshman walking onto campus—the one who thought she needed to have everything figured out before she got to school—here's what I'd tell her:

Call your mom when you don't hit. Give her a chance to help you instead of deciding for her that she can't help. Don't hide. The isolation makes everything worse.

Your self-talk matters more than your batting average. The voice in your head will either be your teammate or your enemy—you get to choose.

Being hard on yourself isn't discipline. Most of the time, it's just making you smaller.

You are not defined by what you do. Your identity transcends your sport. You'll spend four years learning this the hard way.

When you finish playing, what remains is who you've become through the struggles and lessons of your experiences. No matter how your college experience turns out, your hard work will pay off.

That numbness I felt after the last out of my career wasn't because I didn't care—it was because I'd spent so much time worrying about the future and hiding my present that I couldn't access my feelings anymore.

Please don't be me.

THE PATTERN I KEPT MISSING

I wrote this book with two purposes: to make the unknowns known to players going into college, and to show that even without a picture-perfect college experience, you will learn so much about yourself. The hard parts pay off.

I know now: if I hadn't experienced what I did, I wouldn't be able to help athletes the way I do now. Without struggle on the field, I wouldn't know how to connect to those experiencing failure. Without confusion after graduation, I wouldn't have the words I have now.

This is one of my favorite quotes for this idea:

> ***"Hard times create strong men. Strong men create good times. Good times create weak men. And, weak men create hard times."***
> ***– G. Michael Hopf***

When I think of my experience in college, my first reaction would be to describe Freshman Me as weak; she didn't have a backbone. She let small failures dictate how she felt about herself. She let other people's judgment shift how she acted.

Weak Morgan created the hard time of her college experience. If she had been stronger, the times wouldn't have been so hard.

But on the flip side, if the times hadn't been so hard, she wouldn't have learned as much. They wouldn't have made her stronger. The hard experience built the strong person.

But my second reaction is to use a more forgiving perspective: freshman Morgan wasn't weak. She was learning patterns she had never encountered before. She was wrestling with perfectionism, external validation, and mental health challenges she didn't yet have the tools to handle. She was doing her best with what she knew.

If I hadn't experienced what I did, I wouldn't be able to help athletes the way I do now. The struggle built something in me I didn't have before. If you're struggling right now, maybe that's what's happening for you, too. But please—don't do it alone.

WHY I KNOW BEING AN ATHLETE IS A NET POSITIVE

Parents and athletes often ask me if what they're doing is worth it. If the stress is actually too much. If it would be better to compete at a lower level to take some of the expectations off.

Only you truly know what's too much for you. But here's what I know:

You are stronger than you think you are.

The body and mind adjust to the stimulus you give them.

Athletes tend to be successful after their playing days are over because there's a constant battle between the comfort normal people seek and the greatness elite athletes crave. Comfort is associated with being "average," and if you don't want to fall in that average range, you're better off learning how to "handle hard better." Like coach Kara Lawson of Duke women's basketball says, "You don't get rid of hard. You get better at handling it."

When you're used to living as an exception, the way you apply that mindset to life outside of sport affects everything—your reality, your perception of where you fit, what you're capable of.

WHAT TO DO NEXT

If you're a high school senior preparing for college:

- Find *your people* (coach, parent, friend, therapist) you can be real with—not just "fine" with.
- Start practicing better self-talk now, before the pressure intensifies.
- Remember that being recruited means you're already good enough; stop auditioning in your own head.

If you're a college athlete in the middle of it:

- Check in: Are you just surviving, or are you actually present?
- If you're isolating, reach out *today*—even just one text to one person.
- Your experience matters more than looking like you have it together.

If you've graduated and feel lost:

- You're not starting over; you're building on a foundation of resilience most people don't have.
- The discipline that made you an athlete will drive whatever comes next.
- It's okay to not know yet—give yourself the grace to figure it out.

IT'S UP TO YOU TO DO THE REAL WORK

The real game has always been about building character and resilience, and understanding your worth.

Playing sports in college might mean that your priority is that sport, but that's far from the only thing that matters.

Transitioning out of sports doesn't mean losing everything. It's about discovering everything you've built along the way. Your athletic qualities are a foundation for whatever comes next. The same dedication that made you an athlete will drive your success in life.

Whether you become a coach, start a business, or change careers multiple times, who you are will shine through everything you do.

I need you to know something:

You're not the only one who's struggled.

You're not the only one who's felt like you weren't measuring up, who's questioned if you belong, who's wondered if it's all worth it.

I thought I was alone in that feeling during college. I wasn't. You aren't, either.

The stories we don't share are the ones that keep us isolated. The moments we think make us weak are actually the moments that connect us. When I started talking openly about my struggles—the weight gain, the loss of confidence, the confusion after graduation—other athletes started reaching out. They told me their stories. They said, "I thought it was just me."

It's never just you.

When your experience as an athlete comes to an end, your story is only just beginning. I genuinely want to hear it. Connect with me (@morganstuart18 on Instagram) or use the QR code I provided at the beginning or end of this book to share your journey—the hard parts, the messy parts, the parts you don't post about—whether you're still in the middle of it or years removed from competition, whether you figured it out quickly or are still searching.

Share your story because someone else needs to hear it. Share it because keeping it inside makes you think you're the only one. Share it because normalizing the struggle is how we all get through it together.

Thank you for reading this. Move forward with intention. And remember, you don't have to do it alone.

THANK YOU FOR READING MY BOOK!

If you're struggling, you don't have to figure this out alone. The Real Work community has hundreds of athletes who've been exactly where you are—and came out the other side. Join us at therealwrk.com:

I appreciate your interest in my book and value your feedback, as it helps me improve future versions. I would appreciate it if you could leave your invaluable review on Amazon.com with your feedback. Thank you!

THANK YOU FOR READING MY BOOK

www.ingramcontent.com/pod-product-compliance
Lightning Source LLC
LaVergne TN
LVHW090530110826
845146LV00003B/1041

9798901580066